MW01532781

HOW TO TALK TO ANYONE FOR INTROVERTS

EASY GUIDE TO BETTER SMALL TALK AND CONVERSATIONS TO MAKE FRIENDS - BOOST CONFIDENCE AND CONQUER SOCIAL ANXIETY, AWKWARDNESS, AND SHYNESS (BONUS 7-DAY CHALLENGE)

DON'T BE STRANGERS

XINYI XAN

WITH

MARGARET O'CONNOR

CONTENTS

© **Copyright 2023 - All rights reserved.**

The content contained within this book may not be reproduced, duplicated or transmitted without direct written permission from the author or the publisher.

Under no circumstances will any blame or legal responsibility be held against the publisher, or author, for any damages, reparation, or monetary loss due to the information contained within this book, either directly or indirectly.

Legal Notice:

This book is copyright protected. It is only for personal use. You cannot amend, distribute, sell, use, quote or paraphrase any part, or the content within this book, without the consent of the author or publisher.

Disclaimer Notice:

Please note the information contained within this document is for educational and entertainment purposes only. All effort has been executed to present accurate, up to date, reliable, complete information. No warranties of any kind are declared or implied. Readers acknowledge that the author is not engaged in the rendering of legal, financial, medical or professional advice. The content within this book has been derived from various sources. Please consult a licensed professional before attempting any techniques outlined in this book.

By reading this document, the reader agrees that under no circumstances is the author responsible for any losses, direct or indirect, that are incurred as a result of the use of the information contained within this document, including, but not limited to, errors, omissions, or inaccuracies.

SECTION ONE: INTRODUCTION AND FOUNDATIONS

My hands are sweaty. It feels like my heart is a spool of wire, being pulled tighter and tighter until it's ready to snap.

Can they smell me? Did I remember to put on deodorant? Just act normal. Why can't you just *be* normal? What's wrong with me? Where will I sit? Will I make any friends?

It feels like people swarm around me. I feel sick but try to pretend to blend in.

Finally, I sheepishly take a seat in the back corner of the classroom, take out my notebooks and binder, and stare down at my hands. I feel like bursting into tears. As a freshman in college, I was terrified that I wouldn't make any connection and end up lonely and isolated. But I still found myself here again, in the back of the classroom, avoiding eye contact and hoping no one would notice me.

Do you feel this way? Like you're different from everyone else? Maybe you feel like you're not even a person— just an alien trying to pretend to be human.

If you find yourself among the 264 million people who suffer from social anxiety, who think to themselves things like: I'm so awkward, or I have no friends, then rest assured that there is absolutely nothing to be ashamed of! Social skills are just like any other skill you've had to learn (from brushing your teeth to using your phone) and can be practiced and improved!

Imagine being able to attend any social event of your choosing and knowing that you'll be just fine! Small talk before an interview? No problem. Chatting with a random stranger? Naturally. You don't feel fazed by social interactions because you are supported by an extensive network of friends who deeply love and care for you. When you talk, people can't help but feel drawn to your self-confidence. You know that conversations give you insight into life, just like reading a good book. And in this book, I'll walk you through defining and attaining your goals for your dream social life and manifesting this self-confidence!

I (Xinyi, "shin-yee") was born in Kuala Lumpur, Malaysia, and moved with my family to Dallas, Texas, at age seven. My first couple of years in school were a huge struggle. English was not my first language, and entering 2nd grade after skipping almost a year of education due to the move made making friends quite tricky. But even after learning English, I never felt quite at home... anywhere.

Culturally, I wasn't fully American, but when my family and I visited Malaysia, I was painfully aware that I didn't quite belong there either. When it came to my passions, I could never decide on a specific creative outlet or medium to hone—not because of indecisiveness (okay, maybe a little bit), but because I find joy in learning, remixing, and over-complicating mixed-media projects. But before I found pride in calling myself a creative chimera, I was hopelessly lost in how to identify my art and, therefore, myself. And being aromantic meant that I couldn't relate to 99% of the stories represented in pop culture.

In short, I thought I was an alien. *After all, surely, you're not human if you can't understand such a primary human emotion as romantic love, right?*

Instead of romance, I dearly longed for brotherhood and sisterhood, the types of platonic love and chosen family you read about in books. The only problem was my extreme introversion and social anxiety. Even amongst my few friends, I didn't have the confidence to share my thoughts and opinions. How could I develop deep and life-long friendships if I was scared to talk to and connect authentically with others?

I was frustrated and tired of being alone, especially in the presence of people. *What if I tried being honest with my friends? What if I complimented that random stranger?* I began to ask myself.

And that's when I realized: I had nothing to lose.

This mindset shift to vulnerability changed everything. As I began to deepen my existing relationships by showing up authentically, I noticed that I was also slowly building my confidence in interacting with absolute strangers. Gradually, I overcame my social anxiety and began to feel like I actually belonged.

Although there are still days when I want to cancel all my plans or prefer watching a room of strangers from a corner rather than engage, I now also know that I'm capable of connecting with anyone I want, whenever I want. And so can you.

You may not feel like it now, but some things in this world are simply true, whether you believe them or not. One of these things is that *you matter!* Your skill sets, ideas, experiences, and stories are meant to be shared. You will find that by growing in confidence and making the connections you want, you won't simply benefit yourself; every person who gets to hear your story will walk away a little less drained and lonely than before. With confidence, you'll also be able to show up authentically in your relationships. Nothing is better than letting someone see you for who you truly are—imperfections and all—and still finding love and acceptance on the other side.

In a world of 7 billion people, I believe that no one should have to suffer from loneliness. Especially given that loneliness has been shown to increase your risk of death by 26% (Campaign to end loneliness, 2019).

Your power to save lives lies in your very existence. When you converse and connect with others, you validate their stories and identities, making them feel like they belong. And in return, you will feel seen, understood, and loved. That's the magic of conversations.

Ready to create some magic? Keep reading.

———

This book was written in collaboration with Margaret O'Connor, a ghostwriter and middle-school English teacher, who shares this enthusiasm for the magic of conversations and meaningful connections! Thank you, Margaret, for helping stitch words into paragraphs and ideas into stories. The book contains personal anecdotes from myself and Margaret. I hope some of them will make you smile!

CHAPTER 1
YES, YOU CAN!

"It's never too late to become who you were meant to be." —George Elliot

am one of the clumsiest people I know. I knock over books from my desk, my work papers are almost always turned in with some coffee stain on them, and my mother kindly let me know that having spilled wine on my Bible is sacrilegious and I should probably sincerely repent if I want to spend eternity in a pleasant place. I have never in my life met someone as clumsy as I am.

So, the day I decided to learn how to swing dance was momentous. I spent a lot of time stepping on strangers' feet in class, apologizing profusely, and counting under my breath. It seemed to me that something as beautiful and graceful as dancing would always be out of my reach.

But after a few practices of breaking other people's toes, I began to learn. Suddenly, the steps didn't seem so hard—my muscles remembered for me, so I didn't have to keep track. Soon, I was about as good as everyone else in the beginner's class. And, with more practice, I became all those things I thought I would never be—graceful, agile, and a good dancer.

Old dogs can learn new tricks. Uncomfortable? Of course! But there should be no doubt that you can learn how to accomplish anything if you're willing to practice.

It doesn't matter if you're young or old, born with or without privilege; research published by The National Library of Medicine shows that even as an adult, you can train your brain to create new neural pathways. The implications? You have the power to create your identity.

WHAT IS NEUROPLASTICITY?

We know that kids learn how to do new things all the time. Their babbling turns into language as their brains rapidly develop the ability to understand grammatical syntax and vocabulary. They go from crawling to gripping the sides of tables dangerously to walk. Soon, they can stumble into a run, and you're going crazy just to try to keep up with them!

We know that kids' brains have the ability to change; they have neuroplasticity. But we also now know that adults have neuroplasticity as well! No matter how old you are, your brain is capable of neurogenesis—the process by which new neurons (brain matter) are formed.

It's common knowledge that undergoing social stress can affect your emotional and social well-being. But did you know that it can impact your brain's chemistry negatively? An experiment performed by the National Center for Biotechnology Information found that chronic social stress and other difficult experiences in marmoset monkeys and tree shrews lessened neurogenesis of the hippocampus, the part of the brain that aids in building memories and learning (Fuchs & Flügge, 2002). It can wear you down and build negative thought patterns if you're constantly anxious about attending class or parties. Your mind might start to tell you all sorts of lies, such as, *"No one wants to be your friend. You'll feel this way forever. There's nothing you can do to change."*

The theory of neuroplasticity says that if you believe these lies, you'll repeat these thoughts in your mind, reinforcing these neural pathways until these ideas are automatic and seem natural and true. If you've experienced this, know that there is nothing to be ashamed of; this is a natural and human response to adversity.

Fortunately, neuroplasticity also works in the opposite direction. If you divorce yourself from negative thought patterns, you weaken these neural pathways until these ideas become foreign and distinct from your identity. Therefore, understanding how neuroplasticity and neurogenesis work gives you control over which habits and thought patterns you want to develop.

Sure, I still knock over my coffee in my workspace at least once a week. But after a lot of practice, I am now a great dancer. Persistent and deliberate repetition builds new neural pathways in your brain, and suddenly things that used to feel foreign and uncomfortable can be accomplished without even a second thought. In fact, The National Center for Biotechnology Information concluded that "the existence of neurogenesis in adult brains gives hope that even damaged brain regions can be functionally repaired" (Fuchs & Flügge, 2002).

HOW CAN WE USE NEUROPLASTICITY TO OUR ADVANTAGE?

Dr. Caroline Leaf, an esteemed psychologist and researcher, discusses the power of neuroplasticity in her book, *Your Mental Mess*. Dr. Leaf says that the mind is the most significant part of our being, making up 90 to 99% of our person. Her research shows that our thoughts, feelings, and choices affect our beliefs and expectations. Therefore, you can physically reshape your brain by consciously choosing how you feel and think (Leaf, 2021).

In one case study, Leaf took on a 17-year-old female patient a year after a car accident that had put her into a 2-week coma. In a span of 8 months, Dr. Leaf was able to train the patient to use her mind to change her brain. The patient's academic capacity improved from that of a second-grader (a result of the accident) to a genius-level IQ, allowing her to finish the school year, surpassing her peers (Leaf, 2021).

This research does not only impact your social life; it affects every area of your existence! Perhaps you have always admired your coworker's ability to get their work done quickly, your brother's ability to light up a room with his jokes, or your friend's killer talent at pool. Maybe you're like me, tired of apologizing for knocking things over while you walk through the office. Whether you want to be gifted, graceful, or charismatic, regulating your mind and structurally changing your brain can heal trauma, bolster your courage, overcome imposter syndrome, and boost your confidence.

If you ever doubt yourself, return to this chapter and remind yourself—you have the power to become anyone you want to be!

CHAPTER 2
WHY YOU MATTER—SOCIAL HEALTH VERSUS SOCIAL ANXIETY

Now that you know you're capable of positive change and growth, let's talk about why you're worth investing time and effort in bettering yourself.

SOCIAL HEALTH

The loneliest time in my life was when I was a senior in high school. I was working hard to get good grades and spent most of my time at home helping out my mom with my little brothers. I would wake up at six, do my homework, and make everyone else's breakfast before waking up my little brothers, David and Dontavious, to help them prepare for the day. I'd drive us all to school, get off of school, take David to football practice and Dontavious home, help Dontavious with his math homework, and then take him to a different football practice before picking up David. Finally, I would arrive home where my mom was cooking dinner.

I vividly remember one of my friends asking me to hang out after school, and I told her no. I had to take David and Dontavious to football. She asked me again the next day and became angry when I said the same answer, until finally, exasperated, I said, "Football practice is every day!"

I didn't understand how frustrating it must have been for her to befriend me. I was drowning in busyness and didn't have time to have fun.

If I felt this way as a baby eighteen-year-old with every physical need like housing and food met by their parents, then I can only imagine how you might be feeling right now. We often don't feel like we need to be social, and we have excuses like lack of time, energy, or desire. But the truth is, time and time again, research has shown us that human beings need community.

We all understand that we are biologically designed as social creatures. As such, we should pay close attention to our social health, which is determined by the quality and quantity of our relationships. The word relationship here does not simply mean a romantic relationship, even though they certainly tie into our social circle. In this book, whenever I refer to the word "relationship," we are talking about any connection you have with any human being: your romantic partner, professional relationships at work, family, or friends you spend time with outside of work.

Quantity of Relationships

Besides raw numbers, quantity also refers to the different relationships you have in this world. Sure, you have a lot of family members who you're very close to, but maybe you don't have so many friends at school. Or your life might be brimming with friends from work, but after you go home, you find that you don't have anyone to hang out with outside of the office.

If you already have a few very close friends whom you feel like you could call in a pinch, that's fantastic! But if you feel like you don't need to meet anyone else because of your few existing tight-knit friendships, consider why a quantity of relationships is so important!

The first reason is that different relationships bring different benefits to the table. You don't just need a friend with whom you watch trash-reality TV shows on the weekends. You need friends who will challenge you and who can spend time with you on other things that you love. Every relationship that I form brings something unique and beneficial to my life. Some of my friends are very encouraging and always know how to point out what's fabulous about me and my existence. Others are very honest. I don't always want to hear what they say, but I've found through experience that I can always trust their judgment.

Quantity isn't just crucial for variety's sake. It's important that no one person has to be solely responsible for your social health.

I had a friend in high school who was constantly irritated with me when I couldn't spend time with her due to taking on too much responsibility in my home. She insisted that I was her best friend and refused to branch out and meet new people. As such, she would get jealous when I made new friends with other people, constantly tell me what a terrible friend I was for not having enough time with her, and act incredibly manipulative to get me to give her more attention.

Eventually, it all became too much for me. I had to tell her that I needed a break from this friendship. I just couldn't be the kind of friend she claimed she needed.

In retrospect, many of these problems stemmed

from a scarcity of relationships this friend had. If she were willing to be friends with other people, then suddenly, it wouldn't wound her so deeply when I had to say no. She could turn to someone else for attention and quality hangout time.

Quantity is also so important because people, circumstances, and lives tend to be in a constant state of flux. The person you spend the most time with may get married, and suddenly your social health plummets because that person is no longer around as much. Friends disappear from our lives for all kinds of various and valid reasons. But by maintaining several relationships from all different parts of our lives, we protect our social health by always having other friends to fall back on.

Quality of Relationships

When you're looking for a quality friend, you want someone who encourages: the development of new friendships, authenticity, and mutual respect. You'll also want relationships that help you develop healthy boundaries, encourage having fun, and make you feel safe and supported.

We will dive more into each of these attributes that make up healthy relationships in Chapter 7.

· · ·

Why Is Social Health Important?

Science shows that social health is fundamentally tied to mental and physical well-being. These studies show that people with the lowest social events are likelier to die than those with greater involvement (House, Landis, and Umberson 1988). Berkman and Syme (1979) demonstrated that the risk of dying for people with fewer social ties was more than double that for those with more social connections. Social links reduced mortality risk among people who even had medical conditions. According to the Centers for Disease Control and Prevention (CDC), low social health is associated with a ~50% rise in the risk of dementia and raises your likelihood of heart disease and strokes by almost 30%. "Loneliness among heart failure patients was associated with nearly 4 times increased risk of death, 68% increased risk of hospitalization, and 57% increased risk of emergency department visits" (Loneliness and Social Isolation Linked to Serious Health Conditions, 2021).

By not taking care of your social health, you make yourself more susceptible to mobility issues, mental health problems such as stress, anxiety, and depression, and a poor immune system which can lead to chronic disease and cancer. On the contrary, having a robust social circle will increase longevity and quality of life.

SOCIAL ANXIETY

So why does social anxiety exist if being social is part of our genetic code? Social anxiety is a common fear of other people's opinions that we tend to experience when interacting with others in social situations, especially with strangers or new relationships. For example, you may feel totally at home with your family and friends, but you're suddenly uncomfortable and anxious when you go to work and are around your coworkers. I feel comfortable with my husband and brothers because they will still love and hang out with me even if I do something silly. But suddenly, when I visit somebody else's house, I am riddled with fear. What if I do something they think is weird? Are they going to laugh at me once I leave? Where's the bathroom?

The first time I experienced social anxiety was in the 5th grade. My friend's dad scared me to pieces. He was driving me to volleyball practice with my friend. I had a terrible cold and was aching to cough, but for some reason, in my baby 5th-grade mind, I thought my friend's dad might think I was weird or rude. I held in my coughs until tears started streaming down my cheeks.

These situations seem silly in retrospect. You can look back and say, *Well, of course, it wasn't rude of me to ask them where their restroom was,* or *If kids get coughs, it's not a big deal.* But when we're in these situations. Our hands start to sweat, and we get nervous that these people secretly hate us.

Why does this happen, sometimes, without us even noticing?

The root of social anxiety is bound to our desire to fit in. Speaking from an evolutionary standpoint, our social circle determined whether or not we survived. Without a tribe, we were more likely to be killed.

This is different in the modern world. Technology and resources have made it easier to survive independently. So, when we experience social anxiety, it is just our body innately understanding the importance of social ties. Acknowledge the discomfort, but trust that you are safe.

The Heimberg Model

To better understand social anxiety, we must first understand *The Heimberg Model.* The Heimberg Model theorizes that anxiety is generated due to an image we create of ourselves in social situations. In our mind's eye, we see the perception that we *think* other people are making of us.

For example, if I walk into a staff meeting late, I'll imagine myself stumbling in with terrible hair and pit stains and everyone critically judging me. In reality, most people in the meeting won't notice that I've entered the room. They don't care if I'm late, and they're not judging my hair. They're probably busily occupied by other things, such as the meeting agenda or what they're doing after work.

As a middle school teacher, I remember having a study hall of eighth graders in my classroom. It was my first year teaching seventh grade, and I didn't know who the eighth graders were. One of the teachers told me this was a rowdy group of kids, so I ought to be extra stern.

Later, another teacher approached me in a solemn, quiet way.

"Alexa thinks you hate her," she whispered to me as we stood monitoring the hallway.

"What?"

"Alexa, in your study hall. She thinks you hate her."

I wracked my brain. I hadn't even learned these kids' names yet.

"Who's that again?"

"She's the one who's coming in late all the time because she's on lunch duty."

I stared at my coworker, nodded, and decided I'd have to chat with Alexa.

Later that day, I called Alexa to my desk during study hall.

I gave her a lollipop. "Miss Serra told me you think I hate you."

She gave me a shy smile.

"I have never in my life even spoken to you! How could I hate you?!"

She shrugged, "I don't know, Miss."

"Have I ever even said a single word to you?"

"I don't know!" She said, but she was giggling a little bit now.

"Well, I like you just about as much as I can, given that this is the first time I've ever spoken to you in my life. You can go back to your seat."

Now, Alexa lights up whenever I see her, and we chat about her day.

Sometimes, we brew in negative self-talk, and our Heimberg Model is deeply affected by the lies we tell ourselves. *You're just a weirdo. Who would ever want to hang out with you?* These lies are pervasive enough to seep into our perceptions of how other people see us. Suddenly, we're thinking about how stupid we must look in front of the class or in the hallway.

Our anxiety tells us that everyone holds impossibly high expectations of us and we're failing miserably. Fear tells us that everyone is judging us and deciding we can't be a part of their social circle. These thoughts fuel our social anxiety, which fuels the lies that we'll never be accepted. It's a vicious cycle.

Fortunately, social anxiety is a mental process, meaning we have control over it!

Outgrowing Your Social Anxiety

Now that we know where social anxiety comes from let's look at how we can grow away from this destructive mindset.

You Belong!

Frequently, social anxiety is rooted in a belief that you don't belong and reinforced by memories of negative social interactions. If you believe that you don't belong, whether it's to your family, peer groups, or others at work, believe me, you do. You are as equally human as I am. Maya Angelou once said, "I am human. Therefore nothing human is alien to me."

When you start chatting with people from all walks of life, you'll realize how amazingly paralleled our experiences are regardless of age, upbringing, and economic standings. Every person is like a book waiting to be read, holding a story to discover and learn from. And like everyone else, you carry within you a universe of experiences to be shared.

Therefore, by simply existing, conversing, and validating your existence, you inspire this same validation process in others. You will feel seen, heard, and loved, and make others feel equally seen, heard, and loved. As you nurture your social health, you will support the social health of others, fortifying the mental and physical health of you and everyone your life touches, combating all the detrimental effects of loneliness, and saving lives.

––––––––

As you practice some of the techniques in the following chapters, you may feel your social anxiety taking hold. Remember, you are deliberately putting yourself outside of your comfort zone to build your courage and confidence. With time and practice, the fear will fade. So, don't give up!

CHAPTER 3

WHO ARE YOU VERSUS WHO DO YOU WANT TO BECOME?

Most people make friends circumstantially. We go to school and our friends are those who we share classes with. We go to work and talk to the coworker whose desk is closest to ours. Because this is the norm, it may be easy to blame not having good friendships on our circumstances. But we're not here to let life happen to us! If we're learning how to change who we are, we'll also learn how to make friends intentionally.

The following series of thought exercises will require you to do some journaling and inner digging. If you've done a lot of personal development work before, this may be easy. If you've never done deep self-reflection, trust that the process may be slow or difficult but ultimately worth it. Pull out your pen and notebook (or your favorite note-taking app on your laptop), and let's get to it!

You also can ask your friends and loved ones their opinions on these questions. That will be a marvelous way to better understand yourself from your loved one's perspective and show vulnerability in trusted relationships. It is also beneficial to ask if anyone you know is also trying to improve themself. You can suggest this book to them and try these exercises together. The accountability will help boost your motivation to complete these journal prompts and strengthen your relationship with the friend you are exploring these questions with!

WHO ARE YOU RIGHT NOW?

Before you can set goals, you need to understand your starting point. Who are you right now? Understanding where you're at versus where you want to go gives you clarity for bridging the reality you live today and the reality you will manifest. Journal about these questions:

- What does your social life look like right now?
- Who makes you laugh?
- Who makes you feel valued?

- Who do you go to for strategy?
- Who do you look forward to seeing the most?
- Who do you call in a crisis?
- Overall, how would you describe the quality of your closest and best friendships/relationships? Do you feel a sense of deep connection?
- Where do you already make friends easily?

For all the questions above, look at your answers and ask yourself, "Why?" Adding this simple question could help you find patterns between the people you value and the things that make their presence so enjoyable. These patterns could inform you what you want to attract more of into your social life.

Where Do You Make Friends Easily?

When trying to make friends in a location where you're uncomfortable, you could feel especially stressed and come off as inauthentic. Identifying where you already thrive can help you use those locations to maximize meeting new people.

For example, I feel most comfortable meeting new people online because I can filter and feel out if I synergize with someone before I ask them to meet in person. This makes me feel less anxious about building on that connection because I know we already share interests in common!

There are several ways to meet people: at work or school, through a pen-paling program, at coffee shops, the gym, volunteer programs, festivals, team sports, the library, and the list goes on. Hop online and see if any of your favorite sports that you played in high school have a community rec team. Or even better, try out for a new sport! When I first moved to Colorado, I tried out for roller derby but decided I couldn't afford the health insurance!

If you're someone who meets people easier in person, start with places you already go to in public. That can be anywhere from your favorite coffee shop to your workplace. It may be initially uncomfortable, but these places are beautiful opportunities to make new friends.

When I first started as a middle school teacher, I decided I wouldn't talk to anyone at work. *All my energy is going towards connections with the students! Everyone else should just leave me alone!*

This way of thinking leads to a lonely life. Whenever we had time to work in our classrooms, I'd hear other people chatting and laughing while I was alone with the papers I had to grade. Eventually, more through the efforts of my coworker than me, I made one friend, Sam, whose classroom is right next to mine. Suddenly, I had a friend to sit by in team meetings, to chat with before the kids came in, and, most importantly, a confidant to go to when I didn't understand the expectations. Having a friend in my corner at work has made working much more pleasant! Now, I also have Erica, who makes me lattes during our free periods, Lisa, who brings in crockpots full of soup and French bread for our lunches, and Tobias, who stops in now and again to chat about politics. All these people make my job an easier place to be.

After you've met friends in person, you can continually deepen your friendships online. I love commenting on Sam's pictures, and she's constantly texting me whenever her students drive her batty. Doing so has brought our friendship to a deeper level.

A pro tip for finding high-quality friends is to use your existing network of friends to meet new people! Quality friends tend to build connections that you can trust and respect. If you have worked on filtering your group of friends, likely, your friends have also filtered their friend groups to share similar values or interests.

Where Do You Want to Learn to Make New Friends?

Maybe you're good at making friends at your volunteer group but not so much at family parties. Perhaps you want to learn to attend events solo to open yourself to the possibility of meeting people (while meeting others while attending an event with your friend is possible, you make it a lot harder since people are less likely to approach you if they think they'll be interrupting a conversation with your friend). Maybe the location doesn't matter; you just want to learn how to meet friends in any situation!

While most of this book will focus on your private social life, these tools will also apply to professional work situations. As there are already many books on gaining influence in the work setting, I wanted to empower the everyday person to broaden their social life to improve their social health.

THE END STATE

When you get to the finish line, what does your dream social life look like? The one that makes you feel supported and full of life. One where you have so many friends you can hardly keep up with all of them? Or maybe you want a small circle in every context. Consider your goals for all aspects of your social network: friends, close friends, family (blood or chosen), romantic, etc.

If your end state seems far-fetched, don't get discouraged! By deciding what you want from your life, you are already one step closer than most people who don't even know they can plan for a better social life!

Now that you see the starting point and the end goal pick one thing you want to focus on improving *right now*. Choosing one focus you want to work on will help you avoid becoming overwhelmed and help you achieve success in your endeavors.

If you're feeling stuck, these are some ideas for goals you strive for!

Learn How to Start Conversations

Starting conversations can be daunting and difficult, especially if you suffer from social anxiety. Unfortunately, it's hard to develop friendships without them! If you're looking to bulk up your ability to start conversations, check out chapter 4, where I walk you through how to initiate a conversation.

Practice Having Conversations

Practicing the art of carrying a conversation is essential for building connections. Sometimes, when we experience social anxiety, we tend to freeze. But the more you practice, the easier it becomes. And practicing having conversations will also help you become more confident with other anxiety-inducing situations in life.

In section two, we will further discuss how to practice having your conversations.

Know More People

Maybe you're hoping to grow your social circle! Great! In chapter 7, we will go over some practical steps you can take to expand your social network. The quality of your friendships is essential to take care of, but quantity also matters. Wanting to know more people is a spectacular goal for your social well-being.

Deepen Specific Relationships

If most of your relationships are surface-level, deepening some of your friendships is best. This allows you to share your true story, hear the truth of others, and exist in a way that feels most authentic and comfortable to you. Deepening specific relationships in your life can be a challenging and scary endeavor. But once you are truly seen and accepted for who you are, suddenly, you have an invisible armor to protect you from the lies of this world. You know you have something to offer—it doesn't matter what everyone else thinks. Being vulnerable with your close friends gives you the confidence to be yourself, even in the face of social anxiety.

Build a Chosen Family

A chosen family is formed when people nurture, embrace, support, and love one another despite not being related by blood or marriage. A tangible example exists in Okinawa, Japan, a Blue Zone that has repeatedly produced populations of people that live long, healthy lives, often reaching the age of 100. Some researchers believe the Japanese idea of "moai" is responsible for this region's longevity. Moai is a group of lifelong friends who support each other emotionally, financially, and spiritually. Elders in Okinawa originally created this idea to help tribes pool their resources and help those in need. Today, moai is seen as a group of social peers for a built-in, lifelong companionship. Klazuko Manna, who has participated in moai since she was a child, stated: "Each member knows that her friends count on her as much as she counts on her friends. If you get sick or a spouse dies or if you run out of money, we know someone will step in and help. It's much easier to go through life knowing there is a safety net" (Kotifani, 2022).

Building a chosen family means committing to a group of friends for the rest of your life. Doing so is a responsibility. But it assures you that you have people dedicated to having your back no matter what.

Breaking Away from Hyper-Independence

Hyper-independence is a phenomenon that is often born out of trauma and manifests in a firm rejection of any form of dependence. Thought patterns of hyper-independent individuals may resemble something along the lines of, "I don't need anyone for anything." This mindset often hinders the person who suffers from it; they wrestle through life's ups and downs in isolation, even when they genuinely need help and support from others. You might recognize people who suffer from hyper-inde-pendence because they struggle to ask for help, find others "needy," are guarded in relationships, and tend to over-achieve.

*Trigger warning: The following paragraph discusses sexual assault and harassment.

There are two instances from my life that I can remember experiencing hyper-independence. The first was growing up on a swim team with a coach who was a child rapist. The issues were pervasive, and most men I knew on the team did not act respectfully toward women. Although I wasn't phys-ically assaulted, the feeling of the constant threat of harassment followed my twelve-year-old self all the way through high school. I refused to speak to any men in my class or discuss my true feelings with any of my friends. I kept my head down, mouth shut, and went through five years of feeling completely alone.

Sounds miserable, right? It took years for me to admit that I needed help. But once I sought it, I found that healing from hyper-independence healed my depression as well.

Later, when David was paralyzed in a car accident, I learned to lean on my friends. I suffered for two years from a terrible, conditional case of insomnia. I couldn't fall asleep without someone else in the room. Every time I closed my eyes, my heart would start racing, and there would be a voice growing louder and louder in my mind, telling me that something terrible was going to happen in the middle of the night and I'd have to deal with it all by myself. When my roommate was home, I could soothe my body back to rest by repeating to myself, "Marissa is here. If something bad happens, she'll be right there with you."

But on the nights she was out, I found myself staring at the ceiling, hopelessly caught up in fear.

Luckily for me, I was surrounded by friends who cared about me. I was embarrassed and ashamed to ask, but when my roommate was gone, my other friends on the floor opened their doors to me. We would pack my blankets, drag my mattress off my bed, push it down the hallway, and set it up on the floor in their rooms. None of them made fun of me as a twenty-two-year-old adult afraid of sleeping alone. Instead, they created a rotating schedule, so I always had a friend to go to if I needed someone to soothe me to sleep.

Fighting hyper-independence is hard. Often, people who have experienced trauma have spent years convincing themselves that others who ask for help are silly and pathetic. But being brave enough to be vulnerable is a strength, not a weakness.

Those nights I spent on other people's floors, chatting as we fell asleep, forged some of my closest friendships in college. Some nights, I refused to go out searching for help and would simply lay in terror alone until morning. But it turns out everyone needs other people from time to time. Maybe for a listening ear. Maybe just to convince their silly minds that it's time to sleep. Whatever you need, asking for help is not embarrassing or weak. When others lend you a hand, they build their own confidence in their friendship with you. That way, when they need help, they know they can ask you.

Know Which Steps You Want to Take

Knowing your most immediate goals for your social health is essential in deciding your next steps. This way, you can take small steps instead of trying to conquer your dream social life all at once. Assuming you've done the work and picked the one thing you wanted to work on, congratulations! You dared to recognize there is room for improvement and are trying to bring yourself closer to who you're meant to be.

Happiness and Discomfort

"The secret of happiness is freedom; the secret of freedom is courage." —Thucydides

Your journey will be uncomfortable, but you can train your courage. Neel Burton, a medical doctor and author for Psychology Today, talks about the essential quality of courage in creating a happy and healthy life. He writes that knowledge is a necessary quality for freedom. But without courage, people struggle to exercise their knowledge and obtain the freedom they want. If you know a lot about investing but are too scared to risk your money, that knowledge doesn't add up to more money than you had before. You must practice courage to apply your knowledge in the real world.

Therefore, it is imperative that you take action.

Reframing Failure

Since the only way to get better at talking to others and creating connections is by doing it, you have to accept that there will be times when you fail. Life is a giant experiment for you to find and better yourself continually. Each attempt allows you to learn what works and doesn't work for you. But like everything else in life, the more you do it, the better you'll get, and statistically, the more likely you'll meet potentially great friends.

I can't tell you how many embarrassing stories I have from trying to connect with people. Once, somebody tried to give me a fist bump, and I shook their closed fist like a handshake. Another time I thought it'd be all good and fun to swim down to the bottom of the lake and throw mud at a guy just because my cousins and I used to have a blast with that activity when we were nine. I can go on and on. Failure is a part of this life we live.

But understanding your underlying motivator (your *why*) will help you to grow in resilience. Good news—you already know your *why*! If you bought this book, you want to improve your confidence and social health. If you ever feel discouraged, return to chapters 1 and 2 and remind yourself you can do this!

If you ever feel too bad about your awkwardness, just think of the time I rode my bike into a five-foot-tall bush while trying to talk to someone I wanted to be friends with. These things happen. But you're brave enough to try again!

———

After doing all this self-awareness and inner work, you might become hyper-aware of your flaws. Never be embarrassed by who you are! Your identity, personality, and quirks make you exciting and interesting! If you encounter anyone during this journey who cannot respect the person you are, then they don't deserve your time. It doesn't make anyone a bad person; it just means that you two aren't compatible conversationalists. Feel free to set boundaries with anyone who tries to shame you for being your fantastic self.

SECTION TWO: UNDERSTANDING CONVERSATIONS FROM BEGINNING TO END

In this next section, we'll look at every aspect of carrying out a conversation: initiation, keeping it flowing, and saying goodbye.

You've picked a specific goal you want to work on, so you'll want to pay special attention to the information relevant to your goal. However, please read the section in its entirety. Why? Because our brains tend to learn best when we're learning in context. Reading through this section will also give you ideas for future goals once you're happy with your current one!

Is This Section Just Full of Common Sense?

There is a difference between subconsciously knowing something, consciously knowing it, relating that knowledge to your personal life, and applying it to your everyday habits. Even if you know some of this advice or these tips sound like common sense, I'm highlighting them to pull them into your consciousness again.

You may already do some of these things but have never consciously thought about it. By being aware of your behavior and the consequences, you can leverage your base knowledge to make conversations fun and easy.

Also, remember that for some people, starting a conversation is the most challenging part; for others, starting is easy, but keeping it going is difficult! So, take the information as it is relevant to you and empathize with those who struggle with different parts of conversing. Conversation and connection are different forms of collaboration, after all.

———

As you practice some of the techniques in the following chapters, you may feel anxiety arise. You are deliberately putting yourself outside of your comfort zone to build your courage and confidence. With time and practice, the fear will fade.

Think of everyone like a book, full of stories, knowledge, and adventures to share. When you talk to a person, it is your chance to choose your own adventure. You can flip to any page by selecting the topics that interest you and read for as long as you desire. Through the skill set of conversation, you'll be able to learn how beautiful other people's stories are and how to benefit others with your own story.

CHAPTER 4
HOW TO START A CONVERSATION

Whether initiating a conversation comes easily to you or not, it is the first step of any connection. Therefore, remember to be intentional by keeping your goal at the forefront. If you're like me and need to improve at thinking on your feet, you can prepare for the encounter! This will significantly aid you in executing your courageous plans to build connections.

Things to consider when preparing for your encounter:

Physical Health

As everything in life is interconnected, we must pause to highlight the importance of your physical health to your social well-being. When you take care of your nutrition, movement regimen, and proper rest and recovery, you'll have the energy to invest in your social life! If your physical health isn't currently in a state you'd like it to be, that's totally fine! Everything is a work in progress. Just make sure that from an energy standpoint, you feel like you've adequately rested so that you can socialize! Otherwise, you'll enter conversations cranky and ready to pick a fight.

Fashion

Your fashion choices have a huge effect on self-perception. Sometimes we forget when we're in a rush to get out of the house, but your self-confidence increases when you wear something that makes you feel comfortable and authentic. Don't overthink your outfits or stress out over your clothes, but also don't disregard the power of fashion. Remember, you're not trying to impress anyone with your clothes; you're just dressing in a way that tricks *yourself* into knowing what an incredible person you are!

I'm sure you recognize the clothes that make you feel authentic and unstoppable. These are clothes that bring about a sense of happiness and calm. These are the outfits you put on in the morning, and you know that while looking like this, you can take on the world. Whether you already have these power suits in your closet or have seen them on others and want to try them out, dedicate some time to learn what makes you feel good.

This is part of personal development, honing your skill to pay attention to and recognize how you respond to different stimuli. You can find different versions of your power outfit. How I dress to feel confident in swing dancing differs from the confidence I feel in my outfits in the classroom. I often tell my coworkers that I don't own a school-appropriate outfit outside of my work clothes. That's why I still wear dress pants on Jean Fridays!

When I was in high school and decided to do life alone, I didn't care what I looked like. I dressed in hand-me-downs that were too big, kept my hair cropped short, and wore the same striped coat every single day. I had decided that I wanted nothing to do with anyone and said so with my clothes.

Once I got to college, I decided that living life alone was miserable. I started to care what people thought and found myself swimming in social anxiety. I had no practice talking to others, and I was so far behind everyone else!

But what I did know was that when I wore my maroon checkered dress with fall boots, I simply looked fabulous. Suddenly, I could inch a little closer to my true self with the knowledge that I was a cutie. It's not so hard to talk to others when you look in the mirror and see your most beautiful and powerful self smiling back at you.

So, don't underestimate the power of your wardrobe. When you face the lies of social anxiety, it will be one of the many tools in your toolbox to speak the truth back to yourself. Who could think you're a weirdo when you look so nice?!

Having Questions Ready

Social anxiety can be challenging, but preparing questions will help you begin conversations and keep them flowing. Here are some sample questions for different occasions. Feel free to browse this list and add any questions to it you feel are appropriate.

Networking Events

Whether it's an ice cream social at college or a conference for your business, networking events are a great way to make connections. If you're at an event for your profession, ask questions like:

- How long have you been in the field?

- Do you see yourself in this career indefinitely? Or will you shift and try something new?
- How did you get into this field? (AKA. What's your life story?)
- What projects are you excited about?

If it's a networking event for college, you can ask people things like:

- How many courses are you taking?
- What's your favorite part of campus and why?
- How did you pick your major? And what do you hope to do with it after graduation?
- How do you manage taking classes, hanging out with friends, and taking time for yourself? (This is a great way to transition into asking about hobbies)

Parties

Parties can be the worst if you're an introvert. I used to *hate* parties, and all my friends used to joke about my general hatred for parties. If we had a mandatory party to attend at school, all of my introverted friends would find me so we could sneak out together.

These days, I actually love parties. I work too hard to turn down a fun time. You never know when you'll be invited to a party you might want to attend. Even if you're like I was and hate parties, if someone you want to be friends with invites you, you may want to go just to grow your connection with that particular person. So, some questions to ask at parties could look like:

- How do you know (insert name of the person who invited you to the party)?
- What do you do for a living?
- Do you live far from here (the location of the event)? How long have you lived there? (Sometimes, you find out they just moved to town, and you can give them recommendations! Otherwise, if they're native, you can ask if they imagine living elsewhere.)
- What do you do in your spare time?
- What are a few good movies or TV shows you've seen recently? (Asking for favorite movies or TV shows always seems to stump people because it takes them too long to evaluate the library of

things they've watched across their
lifetime.)
- Where would you be if you could be
anywhere right now?

Be Prepared for the Unexpected!

You never know when you'll strike up a conversation with a stranger in line at the cash register at the grocery store or your local coffee shop. Having some general questions memorized for just these occasions might be good. Things like:

- What's your favorite restaurant in the area?
- Have you read any good books lately?
- Tell me about your family, kids, or job.
- What's something good that happened to you today?
- I love your shoes! Where did you get them? (Or other similar compliments)

The Office

These places are lovely areas to meet new people

as you already share something in common. Some questions you can ask in these settings are:

- Are you working on anything interesting?
- How long have you worked here? How did you end up at this company?
- How does your work connect to your passion?
- What are you hoping to accomplish?
- I'm trying to meet more people at work. Is there anyone else on the team (or in the company) that you think I should chat with? If you are trying to develop a specific skill or have a goal in your profession, you can frame this question in the context of that goal or skill set. Otherwise, you can just ask about other people who they think are a joy to talk to!

Online

Meeting friends online is a fabulous way to connect with new and exciting people. Depending on the forum, you can ask questions about similar interests. For example, if you meet in a video game forum, you can ask the players their opinions on the video game you're playing and what other games they'd recommend. If you meet on social media, you can ask them about their hobbies. Creating connections specific to your forum starts your line of questioning at the root of your shared hobbies.

Digital platforms work very well for me because, for some reason, I fear rejection less when interacting online. It may be because of the number of people that I can access. I always think, "If this doesn't work out, there are other cool, kind, funny, and smart people to meet!" Unlike the physical world, I'm not geographically limited to the number of people I can access. The only real barrier is engaging in an actual conversation with someone. Many of the tips in the following chapters also apply to online connections.

Online Interest Groups

Joining an interest group online is a great way to meet people with similar interests. I love chatting with people about books online.

Cold Emailing to Make Friends

Hey, it can actually work! Tell them how you found them, thank them for something they've shared (why you found them), then ask a genuine question to get them to respond! Ask for advice or opinion on something related to their work!

Social Media

When making friends via social media, avoid instantly privately messaging someone. Interact publicly by asking honest questions on their posts that can elicit a response. Instead of telling someone, "I like it!"; try:

- Where did you buy that? / How did you find out about it?
- How did you get into this hobby / career?
- What was the inspiration for _____?
- What was your favorite part of (your trip, this project, etc.)? Why?

Or questions that you think would be interesting or fun to answer. If you get a conversation going, you can directly message them!

If the platform offers (and you've built the rapport to a point where you feel like you'd like to meet this friend in person one day), try sending voice notes or even a video message. It is a sign of vulnerability to share your voice and is another way to break the digital / physical barrier. Try to schedule a voice or video call to have a real-time conversation! And if all goes well, you can ask to meet in person! If you've filtered online for people who live geographically close to you, this will be easier, but a future trip is also something else to consider.

Disclaimer and Note on Safety

I've received countless questions from friends about connecting with strangers online and turning them into real, life-long friendships. Therefore, these are tips that have personally worked for me. I have never had any issues using online platforms because I filter and choose who to speak with, but remember your street-smarts even in the digital world. Know when to back away and block people if something feels wrong. Like everything in life, please take this advice with a grain of salt and experiment, experiment, experiment! Do what feels best for you.

When I first met up with my husband after meeting him on a dating app, I told all my friends where I was. I was scared because my parents had kindly let me know that most people who meet people on the internet are murdered. I even texted my friends his license plate number when he showed up. If you're meeting someone in real life for the first time, meet in public. You can bring pepper spray if you want to. My dad gave me a can of bear spray for Christmas once and let me know that if I could ward off bears with this spray, surely these men from the internet could also be warded off in an emergency.

> **Pro tip:** Share your location! Many messaging and map apps nowadays let you temporarily share your live coordinates with friends and could be a good failsafe. Again, if you're the one reaching out to others, it is unlikely that these measures are necessary. However, this is just a gentle reminder that you can be both welcoming to others and able to protect yourself.

Meeting One-On-One

If it's a one-on-one meeting, feel free to prepare the questions in a notebook or on your phone, and depending on the context, don't bother memorizing them. If there is a lull in your conversation, you can just say, "I wrote down some questions I wanted to ask. Let me take a look…" and it will show the sincerity that you took to think ahead. The person will feel special that you dedicated that time to them.

My husband and I met on an online dating app, and for our first meeting over zoom, he had a word document pulled up on his laptop. He had changed the background in his document to black so I wouldn't notice the screen lighting change in the reflection of his glasses. When I eventually found this document on his laptop after we were engaged, he told me that he was incredibly embarrassed to have questions written down. I thought it was charming, and all my friends told me how lucky I was to have a partner who is so intentional about his time with me. You might feel embarrassed, but if you have something written down, almost always, the person you're meeting with will be flattered that you took the extra step to make the most of your time together.

————

And if all else fails, ask something simple and expected. A simple "How are you?" or "Have you been here before? Are you familiar with this area?" or "How do you know the host?" are all very standard and easy questions to answer. Even better, throw out a compliment. People LOVE to be complimented, and they'll remember your kindness and how you boosted their confidence. Follow up with a positive question: "What's something good about today?" They'll be happy to tell you the good things in their lives.

MAKING THE FIRST MOVE

Taking the initiative gives you control of the situation because you can choose who to talk to. You also make a good first impression by inviting others into your social circle and making them feel like they belong.

First Impressions 101!

If you've done the above preparations, you're already setting yourself up to create a warm and welcoming environment for the people you talk to. Here are a few extra tips to try when setting the stage.

Smile!

This is something that's a cliché for a reason! Smiling shows that you're happy to see this person and gives them a sense of joy. When you smile at your coworkers and classmates, they immediately know you're someone they can say greet and approach.

Remember Their Name

Everyone loves to have their name remembered. Instead of giving you tricks for memorizing names, if remembering names does not come naturally to you, I suggest being honest about it. Give them a heads-up that you'll be asking for their name again in the future. I am very bad at memorizing names and always have to say this to people.

"What's your name again? I am so sorry; I am the worst with names."

They usually laugh and say, "No problem! My name is ____. And remind me what your name is again?"

Give yourself the grace to commit this faux pas by telling people you're bad at this before you forget their name. Even just saying something like, "I'll probably have to ask you at least three times more today before I remember," helps you and the person you're talking to know that you're not being rude. Sometimes names don't stick, and this avoids any awkwardness with feeling like you can't ask again. You can also write down the name somewhere immediately after meeting them, which will also help with memory consolidation. I personally find that setting this expectation upfront is generally a relief for others as well because it permits them to ask for my name again as well. And just as most people would find it heart-warming that you intentionally prepared questions to talk with them, showing your sincerity for learning someone's name through repetition will also make them feel special!

Welcoming Body Language

Here are five posture tips to help you communicate without words that you're excited to get to know people.

1. **Have an open posture.** An open posture is communicated with both your face and your arms. If you're always walking around with your head down, staring at your feet, or standing around with your arms crossed over your chest, you're silently communicating that you don't want to talk. Your body language has power over other people's subconscious minds. They may not consciously think, *Ah! Here's someone who doesn't want to chat!* But subconsciously, a closed posture communicates a desire to be left alone.

2. **Stand up straight!** Standing up straight is excellent for a lot of social reasons, the main one being you'll appear more confident. Folks who stand up straight

with their arms at their sides appear to be at ease in any situation. It will also help you take deeper breaths, strengthening your voice and calming your heart. Standing up straight also forces you into an open posture by keeping your head up and shoulders back.

3. **Make eye contact.** When I worked as a trauma-informed curriculum educator, we would have children who had undergone emotional disabilities play games where they had to make eye contact with their peers. Why? Because eye contact is one of the most research-based tools used to create bonds with others! If you avoid eye contact, people will think they're making you uncomfortable and be less likely to approach you in the future. Meeting their eyes helps them to know you're excited to connect with them!

4. **Gesticulate!** Talking with your hands makes you seem and feel more comfortable and engaged. I try to keep all my liquids away from the desk because if someone stops by my classroom to chat, I immediately start telling stories with my hands and am prone to knock things over!

Using your hands makes you seem more animated and excited to converse.

5. **Remain still!** You don't need to be a statue when you talk to others, but try not to fidget too much. Fidgeting and pacing make you appear nervous and distracted.

SMALL TALK

Why do introverts hate small talk? Jon Baker, an author who helps introverts achieve more in their lives, lists some reasons he despises about small talk. See if you resonate with any of them.

- **Ego**. People love to brag about their accomplishments, and small talk is often a platform to do so.
- **Imposter Syndrome.** You might wonder if you're interesting enough to talk to. Or maybe you're nervous that you're too different. We all struggle with imposter syndrome to some degree.

Just today, I had a group interview with fifteen different candidates. We were all going around saying a "fun fact" about ourselves. I was so nervous and flustered by the time the question got to me; the only thing I had come up with to say was, "When I was a kid, my mom bought peacock eggs off of Craigslist and hatched them in our living room. Our property is full of peacocks. We went tent shopping for them this week so they don't get too cold."

I spent the rest of the interview day wondering what kind of person says that *at a professional interview*. Who talks about their mom's weird hobby in front of fifteen doctoral candidates?! The great thing about small talk is that it's small—whatever you say tends to be forgotten within the next ten minutes.

- **Social Battery Drain.** Small talk might quickly drain your people energy. I relate to this! I don't always want to spend my limited social battery discussing the weather!
- **Not That Interesting.** Or maybe small talk feels too shallow and a little bit fake to you?

While all these are valid reasons for why introverts like us tend to shy away from engaging in superfluous chatting, I want to also propose a mindset change.

. . .

How to Use Small Talk to Filter Who You Spend Your Time With

Focusing on how much you dislike small talk will make it harder for you to be present and keep the conversation flowing. Instead of dreading light conversations, see it as a way to filter people to understand who is worth your time to converse with deeper.

Yes, everyone has a story to share, and there is something you can learn from anyone, but this doesn't mean you should try to connect deeply with everyone. You know what it feels like to leave a social situation drained versus energized. Use small talk to understand a person's energy. Are they generally optimistic or pessimistic? Do they treat your conversation like a collaborative effort and also ask you exciting questions? Do they respect you and your opinions? Do their values or interests align with yours? Once you understand a person's disposition in conversation, you can decide whether or not you want to pursue more vulnerable discussions with them.

RULES AND EXPECTATIONS

These general rules of thumb will help you make initiating conversations much easier!

Trust That You Are Likable

Rule number one in making new friends: trust that you are likable. Now, there's a fifty-fifty chance that someone will like you. So, why assume that everyone you meet will find you to be a wonderful, pleasant person to be around?

Because a fifty-fifty chance is pretty good odds, half of your interactions will be with people who will like you. And, if you have to choose an attitude and leave the rest up to chance, why not side with the attitude of positivity? Assuming everyone you meet will like you will encourage you to converse more confidently. On the other hand, if you expect people to be repulsed by you, then that negativity will ooze from your pores. People will pick up on how you treat your conversation with them, so being optimistic will increase your luck and make it more likely that they'll want to be your friend (Cafarchio, n.d.)!

Have Little to No Expectations

The next rule of thumb is to approach your social situation with few to no expectations. This may seem to contradict the advice above in expecting people to like you. However, trusting that you are likable is something within your realm of control. Whether they like you or not is beyond your control. Wisdom is recognizing that some things in life are simply outside your power of influence.

Will rejection hurt? Of course, it will. But remind yourself that nobody owes you companionship, and you're too much of a valuable asset to other people's lives to spend time with people who don't recognize your value. Sometimes, the gap between your interests, values, and your current stage in life is so great that there isn't synergy between you and this other person. If so, that's life, and it's totally okay!

Question Your Assumptions

Consider what social rules and assumptions you've made about initiating conversation and connections. Now question them. Sometimes, your assumptions are founded, and other times they aren't!

For example, many assume that others don't want to be bothered. You might think people just don't want to chat in the mornings at work! But we also know that every single person is different. Sure, that assumption might be correct for some. But for others, your beliefs may keep you from adding some great people to your social circle!

This fact will vary from day to day for different

individuals. As a middle school teacher, there are some days when I simply don't have the energy to entertain my colleagues. I want to save all my social battery for the kids in my class! I held onto this belief that I needed to conserve my energy until a colleague asked me about my day before the kids came in. Every day, she would pause and ask about how things were going. Even though I was short and persistent in my mindset initially, her kindness eventually wore me down. Now, we're great friends, all because she questioned a once-correct assumption that I didn't want to talk to my colleagues.

Another common assumption is that our connection expires in old relationships, and we feel it would be awkward or strange to reach out after disconnecting for so long. Most likely, the person on the other side of this relationship is just as busy and tired as you are, and they might miss you just as much as you miss them. They likely have withheld from reaching out because they *also* feel it would be weird to do so.

I once had a friend on the swim team who I lost contact with. We had been close for maybe three months when we swam for our high school team for a season, but then we lost touch. When I was a sophomore in college, I hadn't spoken to her for about five years when I heard about her cancer diagnosis. You can imagine how awkward I felt reaching out to her so many years later, but I decided it was the right thing to do. I sent her a message saying, "Hey, I know this is crazy because we haven't talked in forever, but I'm so sorry about what you're going through. I bet you get a lot of messages from people who never talk to you anymore, but I just wanted to say that this sucks, and I'm sorry it's happening."

I thought she would ignore the message, thinking, "*Another acquaintance feels bad enough that they messaged me. Great.*"

Instead, her reply was: "Oh my gosh, Margaret, what are you talking about? I've missed you! We should totally hang out later!"

Don't assume that your connections are like milk. They don't go bad if you keep them in the fridge for too long.

Another assumptive trap you may fall into is thinking that this stranger you're talking with may never become your friend, so why waste your time and energy chatting with them? It definitely won't if you don't even try! I was a hard egg to crack. My coworker who stopped by my room every morning was going out on a limb. Now, we plan on doing jiu-jitsu classes together once I can afford it; I stop by her room almost every day for coffee, and I set her up on a date with one of my other friends! I would say our acquaintanceship has blossomed into a genuine friendship, all because my coworker decided not to give up on me!

Remember, everyone you know in your life was once a stranger to you, including your blood or chosen family. So, starting to build relationships via conversations is something you've done many times before, even unintentionally!

CHAPTER 5

FLOW — HOW TO KEEP THE CONVERSATION GOING

Now that you know how to start a conversation, it's time to learn how to keep that conversation going. Use this acronym FLOW to guide your questions and answers to hold a conversation.

F: FRIEND (TO MAKE A FRIEND, YOU HAVE TO BE A FRIEND)

If you want to talk to people to make deep relation-ships that support your dreams and joys, you must remember that to make friends, you need to act like a friend. As early as step one, when you approach a stranger or cold outreach to someone online, you want to embody the warmth that you wish to receive from a friend.

In chapter 3, you reflected on the qualities of your best relationships. Keep these in mind as you act as a good friend to everyone you talk to.

The following three letters in FLOW are guidelines for acting as a good friend.

L: LOVE

Choose to love this person instead of perceiving them as a threat or someone you need to impress and gain approval from. *Did you know that love is a choice?* While hormonal reactions may initially drive romantic love, all true life-lasting love (including spiritual, platonic, companionable, and familial) is an active choice of how you care for another person, respond to conflicts and challenges, and grow or let die a given relationship.

Fundamental love is composed of 4 different components, all of which require active participation and intentionality: attraction, connection, trust, and respect (Onojighofia, 2020).

Attraction

Attraction is vital for any relationship, even for non-romantic contexts. You don't have to find your friends physically attractive, but you should find their personalities attractive.

How do you know if someone has an attractive personality? Attraction is based on finding value or appeal. For me, I find authenticity to be a beautiful quality in any friendship I have. I cannot pretend to be someone I'm not, and I don't want to be around others who are too insecure to be themselves. It feels off and uncomfortable.

You might have journaled about the attractive qualities of your friends in the earlier chapters of this book. Note that each person probably has differing qualities that appeal to you. You may like that one friend has a great sense of humor while enjoying that another friend shares your hobbies (Reeder, 2012). I love a friend who can have a cup of tea, sit on the couch with me, and watch a nice episode of trash reality TV. You might like people who hike! We're all different, so figure out what you enjoy about your friends and live into those traits.

Connection

Proximity and *similarity* make up the core components of connection.

Physical context, such as living close together or working at the same place, gives you *proximity* to others. This shared context will naturally generate shared experiences to bond over. If you work as a teacher at the same school, you might click over the fact that one middle schooler is always picking their nose. When you grow up in the same family, you might have a connection with your siblings just because they grew up in the same surroundings.

I once had a conversation with my sister about our connection. We decided we probably wouldn't be friends if we hadn't been sisters. We have nothing in common! She loves to hunt. I like writing. She's an extrovert. I tend to be very introverted. We are two totally different people, yet, we're excellent friends. Why? Because proximity has made our connection strong! Even though the only thing we have in common is the family we grew up in, we can spend hours just chatting through those experiences. As the years have passed, we've found that we have more and more in common.

Proximity often lends itself to *similarity* as it creates experiences you can share. *Similarity* is simply what you have in common. Are you of the same values, beliefs, hobbies, or field of career? Great! You have the foundation to build a strong connection (Onojighofia, 2020).

Trust

Trust is essential for any given relationship. If you can't trust someone, you'll unlikely be friends with them for long. If you act untrustworthy (sharing private information, gossiping behind someone else's back, or saying you'll show up and then not coming through), then it's unlikely that your friends will want to remain friends with you in the future. Trust is essential for love, and it has to be earned. While watching to see if your friends earn your trust, you can do everything you can to earn theirs (*A Few Requirements for a Strong Friendship*, 2020).

Respect

Respect is a fundamental act of love. When you show respect, you will naturally also build trust. If someone disrespects you, don't feel obligated to stay friends. You don't need anyone in your life who makes you feel bad about the person you are. Don't let others poke fun at the things which are important to you. If somebody hurts your feelings, let them know. If they apologize and try not to do it again, you know this is a real friend who truly cares about you. But if they roll their eyes and tell everyone that you're too sensitive, maybe it's time to move on (*What Is Respect in a Healthy Relationship? - Love Is Respect*, 2022).

. . .

How to Choose to Love a Person

Do you know what they say about how love is like wearing rose-colored glasses? You only see the best parts of this person and easily overlook their flaws. While we're not suggesting that you ignore red flags or force yourself to put up with personalities that you dislike, you always have the choice of focusing on a person's highlights instead of their shortcomings.

When you lead with love, you'll naturally create a positive feedback loop where your love generates a positive response in the receiving party, encouraging you to love them more deeply. That's why it's crucial to choose love and communicate it so that the other person can receive and return the good energy.

Show Your Gratitude

An easy way to generate love for someone (even with strangers) is to practice gratitude with them! If you appreciate something about someone (whether it is a piece of advice they gave you, the fact that they're spending time with you via conversations, or the courage they demonstrated in a story they shared), tell them! It can be during a conversation or following up with a text, voice message, or written note. You never know how much you can make a person's day with a small compliment; it'll feel good for you, too (*Gratitude: The Simple Way to Make Your Relationship Better and Happier | Toucan*, n.d.)!

Note that as you're giving praises, pay attention to any compliments you receive in return. Save them somewhere that you can always refer back to! This will provide a little boost of encouragement for your self-esteem and self-confidence whenever you need it!

Speak Their Love Language

Beyond giving direct compliments, you can demonstrate your love for a person using their own love language. The five love languages are w*ords of affirmation, quality time, receiving gifts, acts of service,* and *physical touch* (Chapman, n.d.).

Words of Affirmation

If someone's love language is *words of affirmation*, they might light up when you compliment them, often compliment others, or you might notice that they keep every nice note they've ever received. Does anyone come to mind? If so, try giving them compliments, positive affirmations, and kind words. You could even try sending them a written note or card. Remember to avoid criticizing or verbally making fun of them.

I am a *words of affirmation* person. You'll be shocked at how far a nice note will go! My journal is full of nice notes people wrote me in college, taped and paperclipped all over the pages. I even kept a note that said, "Thanks for lending me your book! You're the best!" *Words of affirmation* friends love a nice little card (With Love, 2019).

Quality Time

A *quality time* person might ask you out for coffee, hang out in your office during work, or just want to spend time with you. You can show some love to *quality time* friends by having one-on-one chats with them. Block out a little of your schedule to ensure you're not interrupted! Don't be distracted, texting other people or working, and take time to truly focus on that person. You can do activities with this person, such as a shopping trip or a meal. Avoid long periods of being apart from a quality time person, and prioritize your time with them. Your action item for this person is to take a walk with this person or plan a day together!

Receiving Gifts

A person whose love language is *receiving gifts* might get you a cup of coffee every now and again or offer to pick you up something from the gas station when they go. I knew my coworker, Lisa, was a love-by-gifts person because she kept bringing crockpots of soup to school and inviting me for lunch. For a person whose love language is receiving gifts, get them a present on special occasions or even on a random ordinary day. These gifts don't have to be extravagant! If they like stationary, it could be a pen you found that made you think of them. If they love food, it could be a box of snacks you saw at the store. Ask when their birthday is, and mark it on your calendar, so you remember to get them something!

Physical Touch

A *physical touch* person will be likely to give you a hug or a pat on the back. To communicate with a *physical touch* friend, use nonverbal cues. Let your potential friend initiate a physical cue first before you do. That way, you don't come on too strong with the hugging. Once you know someone loves a hug, don't be shy with them.

One of my strongest memories of college is

making friends with Katie. I am not really a physical touch person, but Katie was! She told me my hugs were like her grandmother's and always asked for one. I loved Katie and wanted her to know these things, so I always obliged. Since we became friends, I've become a better hugger to everyone because I like to think I hug just like Katie's grandmother.

If you find yourself amongst those trained by society or upbringing to reject physical touch (commonly found in American culture or a consequence of social isolation after COVID), consider changing your perspective (*Most of Us Are Touch Starved | Psychology Today*, n.d.). As part of our social creature biology, we carry touch-sensitive receptors known as C tactile (CT) afferents which can be found across almost every part of our skin. These nerves respond specifically to the caress of another human, as shown by their strong reaction to gentle touch of around 32C (body temperature).

Neuroscientist Helena Wasling Ph.D. says that these nerves are distinct from other receptors on your skin that detect general touch because they directly communicate with the insular cortex, "a deeper part of the [brain] that deals more with your emotional equilibrium." In the case of positive physical contact, these nerves will tell your brain, "'That was nice. I'm accepted. I feel safer now. Someone is counting on me.'" (Halton, 2022). Even if *physical touch* is not your preferred love language, find small ways to incorporate it into your social interactions. This could be as simple as hugging your friends when you greet or say goodbye to them! Your brain will thank you.

———

Of course, you should also learn your personal love languages (the ones you want to receive), but when showing love, you want to remember the love languages of the receiving party. If you love to receive gifts, but your friend prefers quality time, it could cause a misunderstanding if you always send gifts to this friend but never spend quality time with them. They could see *gift giving* as a "cheap way out of spending quality time" when that is not your intention.

Self-Love

Note that everything mentioned above can also be used on yourself. Instead of choosing criticism when you speak to yourself (because we can be our own harshest critics), choose gratitude! Give yourself words of affirmation. Recognize that you also need quality time with yourself.

Self-love is key to self-confidence. When you love yourself, you will naturally have more love to share with others. So, when you work on improving your relationship with yourself, you'll get the added benefit of improving your relationships with everyone else!

Training Your Emotional Intelligence (EQ)

What is emotional intelligence? And why is it important? Emotional intelligence is a person's ability to identify and manage emotions while reacting to the emotions of others (Martin, n.d.). This kind of intelligence helps you perceive what others are feeling, use your emotions and competencies to relate to others, and manage your reactions to these situations. Researchers have found that having high emotional intelligence is associated with many positive outcomes, such as:

- Increased mental and physical health (feeling overall more optimistic about life)
- Better relationships (greater cooperation and satisfaction)
- Increased work performance (leadership roles, productivity, and higher income)

Lucky for us, studies have shown that it is possible to increase your emotional intelligence (Schutte et al., 2013). Use the following tips to increase your EQ.

1. Observe your feelings. Our society tends to value productivity above everything else. We've been told that success is equated to making a lot of money, buying a lot of stuff, and filling our time to the fullest capacity. When we are constantly planning and doing things, it can be tough to pause and try to think about how we actually feel.

Last year was my first year as a full-time middle school teacher. I caught COVID, and while locked away in my home, I got bored and applied to a bunch of master's programs for writing. I was accepted and discovered the school I work for could pay for my entire education! But their grant that could pay for these things expired in eight months. So, what did I do? You got it! I completed a two-year program in eight months while working full-time, like an *insane* person.

I had no idea how miserable I was until my husband gently let me know. I was crying one day, and he finally said, "Margaret, I wish there was just one day when you didn't feel so sad!"

I was totally stunned. I had no idea I had cried every day that week.

It can be shockingly difficult to notice how you are doing emotionally. You can try setting a daily timer. Take a few deep breaths whenever it goes off, and check in on yourself emotionally. How are you feeling? Pay attention to your emotions and what's going on inside. You could even practice journaling about it (Martin, 2022).

2. Take note of the relationship between your emotions and behaviors. Pay attention to how your circumstances affect your feelings and how you react to those feelings. You might notice that you get cranky when you're feeling angry. When I feel sad, I tend to hole up in my PJs, sit around, and watch TV. When you acknowledge your emotional triggers, you can decide how to react to this sudden burst of emotions (Martin, 2022).

3. Own your emotions. Recognize that you are in control of how you feel. Often, emotions arise as directed by what we think about a situation. When someone cuts me off while I'm driving on the highway, my initial reaction is irritation as I think, "How rude! Was that necessary?" This is often followed up with a second thought, "What if this person is in a hurry for an emergency? A personal matter of life and death?" This dual perspective almost always alleviates any internal turmoil, as I forgive this stranger for the potential emergency they may be dealing with. I decide whether this situation is severe and something worth mulling over or minor and forgettable (Martin, 2022).

Sometimes some circumstances are traumatic enough that it feels impossible to control and change your emotional reaction. A typical example of this is the fallout of a romantic breakup. Even in these circumstances, you can acknowledge your feelings, honor that these emotions are valid, and take action to elevate and change your mood. While this may take weeks, months, or years to heal from, when you take responsibility for your emotions, you don't let these negative situations permanently ruin your life. Even as you may encounter emotional breakdowns whenever the wound is fresh, you seek help by confiding with loved ones, moving your body via walks or exercise to generate dopamine (your feel-good hormone), and doing things you love to recover your mental state. Once you've re-stabilized your optimism, you can evaluate your situation more rationally and clearly define how you want to proceed with life (for example, try dating again or enjoy your newfound single lifestyle!).

When you act in a way that you don't like because of unpleasant emotions, deliberate on how you will behave next time you experience similar feelings. By repeatedly and consciously choosing your emotional reactions to certain situations and triggers, you will direct neuroplasticity processes in your brain to change your natural response until you will no longer have to consciously decide.

I used to isolate myself when I felt down. Now, I know that it's actually better for me to see my friends and social circle, so instead of numbing out with social media, I text everyone I know to see who's free for brunch. I call my long-distance friends, go to my little brother's house for a movie, or spend some extra time chatting with my friends at work.

Empathy Versus Sympathy

There needs to be more clarity between sympathy and empathy as these terms are often used interchangeably. However, it is essential to note that they are distinct behaviors of how we relate to someone else's situation. Recognizing this difference can significantly elevate your EQ.

Sympathy is an external perspective on a person's situation. Instead of stepping into the shoes of a person's circumstances, you respond to this person's tough situation as an outsider looking in. A person who approaches someone's story with sympathy often thinks they are happy they're not dealing with this person's situation themselves. Sympathy avoids personal emotional engagement.

Empathy, on the other hand, requires emotional expenditure. You feel what the other person feels, whether by recalling a memory of a parallel situation you have experienced or simply understanding the circumstances from their perspective. When you approach someone with a heart of empathy, you're not looking to judge that person and how they cope with their stress. It is often more powerful than sympathy; however, it can be emotionally draining to approach all situations intending to take on your friend's feelings. Experiment with both and see what works best for you in different circumstances.

O: OPTIMISM

What is optimism, and how does it help with connection? Optimism is a mental posture of hope and confidence. Optimistic people tend to view hardships as opportunities for learning and growing. Even on their very worst day, an optimist can say, "Tomorrow will be better."

If you've ever been in a conversation with another person and felt a shift in your mood, you've experienced co-regulation—a bidirectional neurological process of individual nervous systems influencing each other (R., 2021). Your optimism can positively impact a conversation's mindset, attitude, and collective energy. And the opposite is also true with pessimism and negativity. While most referenced studies of the strong relationship between optimism and productivity are tied to the workplace, optimism and positivity in our day-to-day lives also produce productive conversations by building connection, trust, and respect (Murphy, 2015).

You can practice optimism by genuinely appreciating, praising, and searching for similarities in another person. As it turns out, most people tend to have more in common than we think. You could find similarities you share between your families, years of schooling, work, hobbies, or hometowns. Even if there are not many parallels in your experiences, can you find anything you appreciate about your conversation partner? I am personally drawn to examples of courage, compassion, and curiosity, so I love hearing stories that reinforce these characteristics. By searching for similarities, we are also actively building empathy and connection.

W: WONDER

Go deep often and early, and enter your conversations with open-minded curiosity! This will keep the questions coming, leading to engaging, meaningful, and deep conversations.

Here are some ideas for how to stay curious in conversations.

Be an Active Listener

Have you ever been conversing with a group of people, and someone talked over what you were saying? You falter into silence and look down at your hands, your cheeks becoming hot. And then, there's that one hero who makes eye contact with you and nods along to your story, encouraging you to pick up and continue on. Be that person! Everyone has something important to contribute to a discussion and deserves to be listened to.

We all know the feeling of talking to someone who isn't listening. Their eyes are unfocused; they glance down at their phones or nod and pretend to respond. This lackluster listening often feels disrespectful.

Research shows that, as a species, we could all be better at listening. Active listening is the conscious effort to understand the complete message of what is being communicated. It will help you develop empathy and lessen your likelihood of encountering misunderstandings and conflicts (MindTools | Home, n.d.).

You can practice active listening by looking at the speaker, putting aside distracting thoughts, and not obsessing over what you'll say next when the other person is talking. Take note of their body language and respond to their stories! You can do this by nodding, smiling, leaning slightly forward to show engagement, or using verbal cues like "Yes!" and "Mh-hm!" (MindTools | Home, n.d.).

It's also essential to ask for clarification. When you listen to a story, you bring your experiences, beliefs, and biases to the table. Your brain automatically filters anything you hear to fit into or contradict your worldview (known as confirmation bias). This can sometimes cause misunderstandings. If you provide feedback to the person talking, you'll clarify what's being communicated as the story is being told. Say things like, "I'm hearing you say..." or "If I understand correctly..." then finish the sentence by retelling them what you just heard them say. This allows them to correct you if you misheard something and, in doing so, show that you're interested in truly comprehending what they're saying.

On the other hand, interrupting someone can frustrate or hurt them. If you accidentally interrupt because you're so excited about a topic you can't help but blurt something out, that's a good sign! Just make sure you loop back to them, so they feel respected by saying, "Sorry, as you were saying… please continue…." If you want to interrupt because you disagree with them, try to hold back and listen to them until the end before interjecting your opinions. Waiting for them to finish speaking also allows you to actively listen to the full context of what they want to convey. If you still disagree when they're done talking, don't be afraid to share your opinions, but do so respectfully. Always be honest, open, and kind.

Ask For Stories

Hearing a story about a person's life is one of the best ways to build empathy with someone.

Our brains love a good story. Uri Hasson, a professor of psychology at Princeton, tells us that storytelling is one of the best ways for our brains to find similarities. When we listen to the ebb and flow of a story, our brain's chemistry starts to resemble the chemistry of the person telling that story and synchronizes our minds (McMurray, n.d.)!

If asking for stories feels unnatural, here are some questions you can try that will lead to a story being shared!

- So, how did you two meet?!
- Where are you from, and how did you get here? (They can interpret this however they want!)
- Tell me a little bit about your family or pets!
- What was something interesting that happened the last time you were on vacation?

These kinds of questions are open-ended, leaving the person you're chatting with an opportunity to jump into crazy tales about their lives.

What's Your Opinion?

Ask for other people's opinions! Everyone loves to chat about their thoughts on things. Of course, you can keep questions light and generic. Ask them about pop culture, like movies or TV shows, major events or holidays that just occurred, or even just their thoughts on certain foods or beverages.

But to make deep, meaningful connections, you should get a little vulnerable and ask them for opinions on subjects and topics that align with your soul. For example, as an Asian American, I felt lost and confused about my identity for most of my life. I constantly ponder, "What is home to me?" and "How does culture impact our identities?" When I feel that someone would be receptive to a deeper conversation, I love jumping on the opportunity to get another perspective on what "home" means to them or what parts of their cultural upbringing formed their identity today.

VULNERABILITY

Vulnerability is the most potent form of curiosity. In her book, *Daring Greatly*, Brené Brown (Ph.D. research professor from the University of Houston on the field of vulnerability) describes vulnerability as "uncertainty, risk, and emotional exposure." It is the curiosity for "what will happen if I show up authentically, flaws and all?" and the courage to do it anyways. Vulnerability is the essence of deep connection and the "center of meaningful human experiences" (Brown, 2012).

Brené Brown's research showed that there is only one difference between people who find solid connections and love and those who don't. It doesn't matter if you grew up in a family without love, have faced trauma, or found yourself in circumstances that make it difficult to meet people. Those who find love are those who believe they are loveable. They tend to be the first to say, "I love you... I miss you," and, "Let's grab drinks after work sometime!" If you believe you are worthy of these connections, you'll be more willing to invite them into your life.

How do you make yourself believe these things? Choose to accept them! If you refer back to Chapter 1, you will recall that we have the power to drive the creation of new neural pathways. By practicing positive self-talk, keeping a gratitude list of things you love about yourself, and collecting compliments you receive from others, you will begin to adopt the idea that you're worthy of love. Once you have the foundation of self-love, you're ready to practice vulnerability.

Asking someone to spend time with you runs the risk of rejection. If you ask someone to hang out, they may say, "Oh, I'm busy..." or, "Ummmm, nah I think I'm good." I can't guarantee you won't meet these responses while searching for connections. But without the vulnerability and courage to ask, you'll never be able to grow these friendships. And without self-love, these sorts of rejections could hurt tremendously.

Myth: Vulnerability is a Weakness

Despite how essential vulnerability is for building

connections, we have developed an enormous distaste for it.

Why do we fear vulnerability? Fear of exposure can stem from many experiences. If someone regularly faces rejection at their jobs, trying to find connections, or in intimate relationships, they may be weary of putting themselves out there again. A fear of vulnerability can also be caused by abusive relationships or growing up in a highly critical family. Such things can impact a person's mental health and self-esteem, leading to a fatal fear of vulnerability that will negatively impact their social health.

It doesn't help that western society promotes hyper-independence, which reinforces the myth that vulnerability is a weakness. By cutting off vulnerability, we also close the doors to love, connection, and intimacy. Therefore, it is vital to practice vulnerability often and early. If you enter a new friendship hiding your true feelings, opinions, and thoughts, it may be even more complicated later down the line to change your disposition. However, this shouldn't deter you from becoming vulnerable with any existing relationship you want to deepen.

How Do We Practice Vulnerability?

We can practice vulnerability by living with

courage and being okay with rejection and failure. We've already discussed the importance of "failure" and how to shift your mindset, so if you need a refresher, peep "Reframing Failure" at the end of Chapter 3!

One simple way you can strengthen your courage is by trying new things! From traveling to a new place to eating a dish you thought you'd never try, there are small everyday ways to practice pushing yourself out of your comfort zone so that you get used to being slightly uncomfortable. Growth is always on the other side of fear. When you build up your courage and tolerance to the unknown, it'll become more effortless to take risks with vulnerability in your relationships too!

Another way to practice vulnerability is by asking people for advice or help! Recognizing that you're feeling overwhelmed or need a right-hand man to overcome a challenge is the first step to fighting hyper-independence. Seeking help is a vulnerability because you must confess that something is wrong and outside your control. Nobody likes being wrong, powerless, or a bother to others. But research has proven that people generally love helping others out. Through fMRI technology, we can now see that helping others activates the same pleasure centers of a person's mind associated with good food and sex.

Helping others is connected to living a happier, wealthier, more productive, and more meaningful existence. Asking for and receiving help builds trust and connection because you admit you are human, giving your friends and loved ones permission to confide their flaws with you in return and seeking your help in the future (Santi, n.d.).

You can also be vulnerable by telling people what they mean to you, especially if you feel they've significantly impacted your life. Do you feel like you've found a sisterhood or brotherhood with someone? Tell them! Is this person potentially your best friend? They should know!

Being vulnerable means being true to yourself and trusting that people will love and understand you. And if they can't accept who you are, vulnerability encompasses the courage to believe you'll find others who will.

What Is Vulnerability Not?

Be careful to avoid becoming an over-sharer on your quest for vulnerability. Don't offer every juicy information about your life to anyone with ears! Let people earn your trust before you tell them about your family trauma, personal aches and desires, and your guarded information. Telling people too much too soon can seem needy (Young, 2020). Let yourself get close to someone before you share your deepest, darkest secrets.

———

In summary, the bulk of keeping a conversation flowing is asking questions and listening well. If you don't like talking that much, don't worry! Let others do the talking for you! When you treat everyone you meet as a friend (F) by showing them love (L), optimism (O), and wonder (W), you'll naturally generate exciting, positive, and bonding conversations!

CHAPTER 6
SAYING GOODBYE

W hether your conversation was easy-breezy or a total flop, all things must come to an end. In this chapter, we'll discuss how to conclude a conversation gracefully, whether you need an emergency escape from a terribly boring or awkward chat or leave a smashing impression to seal the deal for a follow-up hangout.

WHEN TO END A CONVERSATION?

Here are some ways you can know it's time to leave:

- The conversation is interrupted in a way that can't be continued
- You or your conversation partner is getting bored

- There's nothing new left to add or keep conversing about
- You need to socially recharge and take a break

When meeting a new potential friend for the first time, I try to set a hard end (typically around 1-1.5 hours) and say that I have another obligation right after (even if I don't have one). If the conversation goes really well and I can spend an extra hour or two with this person, I always have the option to cancel or reschedule the "obligation" on the spot. Set the time limit to whatever you're comfortable with. If carrying on a 1-hour conversation with a stranger is exhausting, try only 30 minutes.

Alternatively, consider ending a conversation early, even if there is more left to explore between you and whomever you're chatting with. *Leaving a good conversation just as it's picking up?! Are you crazy?!* Science says this is how we optimize our joy – by having something to look forward to. Humans are incredibly future-oriented, as planning is one capacity that distinguishes the human brain from its animal counterparts. This is observed through the power of anticipation.

A recent study exploring the correlation between happiness and vacations found that it doesn't matter how long you vacation for or how much money you spend on your vacation. Vacationers aren't joyful because they get more rest or have experienced more adventures. They're happier because they have times in their year that they can look forward to. Therefore, anticipation is tied deeply to happiness (Nawijn et al., 2010).

Anticipation is also correlated to optimism, which helps combat stress and depression. Leaving a conversation as it picks up can leave a powerful and positive impression. Not only are you giving your conversation partner a reason to want to chat again (because there's still so much more to talk about!), but you end the interaction on an energetic high. This increases the likelihood that you and your friend will want to schedule a follow-up hangout.

Fun fact: You can also use the power of anticipation to make other parts of your life more enjoyable! Next time you're working on a large task or project, instead of working until you're bored or stuck before taking a break, take a break as you're making good progress and feel like you're on a roll. This will make it easier for you to pick up the task again and keep going, as you have something to look forward to when you return!

HOW TO END A CONVERSATION

Different techniques for ending a conversation will apply to different scenarios. Try a few of these ideas when saying goodbye, and see what works best under varying circumstances!

Pivoting to the Future

When it's time to end a conversation, you can make a nod to the future by saying something like, "Do you have anything fun planned this week/weekend?" This shifts the conversation from the present or past tense into the future tense. This can be followed up with, "It was great talking to you! Good luck with that interview you have tomorrow," or "It was so fun chatting with you. Enjoy your relaxing weekend!"

This is my favorite way to end a conversation and something I was already doing naturally without realizing it! This applies to almost all interactions because you can say something as simple as, "What are you up to after this?" It gently tells your conversation partner that you're mentally preparing for the end of the chat and ready for the next thing in your day!

Give the Other Person an Excuse

With this technique, you politely acknowledge that your conversation partner has other tasks to take care of. This looks like: "I'll let you get back to what you were working on. Thanks so much for chatting with me." Or if you're at a networking event or party, you can say, "It was great meeting you. I'll let you go so you can chat with others!" Or, more generically, for any occasion, "I'll let you get back to your day. Thank you again for the lovely conversation."

Create an On-The-Spot Time Limit

If you didn't enter the conversation with a time limit set, inventing one while the conversation is rolling is always possible. You can say, "I just remembered there's something I need to take care of in 30 minutes, but until then, I'm totally down to chat."

If you have less than half an hour to spare, this also works for shorter timeframes. Suppose you get caught unexpectedly in a conversation with your coworker and need to return to your job. You can say, "I need to get going in about 10 minutes to complete a task." This avoids abruptly ending the chat.

On a more general occasion, say, "I need to go in about five minutes to get back to work/catch a class/meet a friend, but I learned so much from the stories you shared."

Schedule the Next Hangout!

You may have enjoyed that conversation so much that you can't wait to see this person again! Instead of waiting to discuss plans over text, figure it out on the spot. It's similar to pivoting to the future, but here you intentionally create your future together!

Say something like, "It was such a blast chatting with you! I'd love to hang out again. Are you free anytime next week(end)?"

Well… How Did That Go?

Whether you had a refreshing and life-giving conversation or a total disaster, at least you tried! In taking the courage to initiate or deepen conversations, you are rewiring your brain and altering your identity into one who takes risks and converses vulnerably!

Keeping the specific goals you've set from Chapter 3 in mind, how connected do you feel to this person after your conversation? Why? What went well? What didn't go so well? Journal about it so that you can observe patterns about your feelings on the topics discussed, your reactions to different parts of the conversation, and how you can improve next time.

. . .

What Now?

If you enjoyed your conversation and feel that there is potential to develop a meaningful connection with this person (whether they could be a potential mentor in a skill or niche you're interested in, a friend you can share hobbies with, or just someone with whom you would confide in for interesting conversations), that's fantastic! In the next section, we'll dive deeper into how to build meaningful and lasting relationships.

SECTION THREE: RELATIONSHIPS

Now that you've established your foundations with self-awareness and participated in a conversation or two, we transition into the most crucial element of elevating our social health – creating meaningful connections.

Building relationships takes time and is like planting a garden. The more time and care you put into your garden or social network, the stronger the plants or relationships will grow. The more seeds you plant (conversations you start with different people), the more you increase your chances of having a bigger harvest (deep friendships).

Sometimes, your garden grows weeds, or your harvest becomes infected. Your relationships feel difficult due to natural misunderstandings or conflicts that arise. But don't become discouraged! I'll walk you through how to avoid and resolve disputes. Overcoming these conflicts will strengthen your bond and boost your confidence that you can handle other challenges in life!

Remember, when you build strong, dependable, and lasting relationships, you're not only fortifying your own social and physical health for a longer and more joyful life. You elevate the quality of life and longevity of everyone you meet and create a bond with.

How incredible is that?

CHAPTER 7

BUILDING AND DEEPENING RELATIONSHIPS

Before discussing how to deepen our relationships, we must first understand the four stages of friendships. You may have experienced these different stages unconsciously with various relationships you have; often, school or work environments move us through these stages for us. However, consciously recognizing these stages and placing your relationships on this scale allows you to deliberately advance certain relationships to feel deeper connections towards certain people!

THE FOUR STAGES OF FRIENDSHIPS

In each of the following stages, I share my personal perspective on what I consider a stranger, friend, close friend, or chosen family. This is just to give you ideas for how you could potentially define these stages for yourself. After having interviewed many strangers and friends alike on my podcast Don't Be Strangers on the question, "How do you define a stranger? And at what point do they transition from being one to not being one?" I've found that these definitions vary significantly based on personal preferences. Therefore, use these stages as a guideline to create your own hierarchy for friendship development.

Stranger or Acquaintance

All friendships start with a stranger or acquaintance. These are people who you share facts with because trust is still low. They have yet to earn a right to your personal life, but there is potential to grow the confidence you have for them. Your common interests are unknown, and the number of acquaintances you can keep in your life is unlimited.

Whether or not you communicate with strangers easily is partially due to your personality. Some people find talking to strangers easy because they don't fear judgment from people they don't know. If you're like me, you care a lot about what strangers think, which might be challenging.

Unless I take the time to have deeper conversations with my coworkers, I usually consider them acquaintances because we communicate on an as-needed basis to exchange facts about our job. I also meet a lot of acquaintances from workshops I've attended where our communication is scoped to the class topic.

Peer Friend

A peer friend is someone you have built a little bit of trust, with whom you have found that you have something in common. They may hear a little about your wishes, dreams, and goals, and you can start disclosing your opinions. You can have several peer friends, and communication with them might be semi-difficult because the boundary lines are less defined.

For me, a peer friend is someone I would want to chat with one-on-one at least every once in a while. When we catch up, we exchange facts about our lives and things that have happened or are currently happening. Occasionally, these recounts of our lives lend themselves to conversations about goals or dreams based on current projects that may lead to these ultimate outcomes. I enjoy their company but don't seek to stay in constant communication with them. I also am okay with encountering them in group settings more frequently (such as a class, club, or a friend reunion).

Close Friend

A close friend is someone who you have developed quite a bit of trust with. You have disclosed some of your weaknesses and vulnerabilities with them. They know about your values and goals. The number of close friends you can maintain is much less than peer friends. Communication is easy and comfortable as you are mutually aware of boundaries.

Personally, I like to stay in relatively frequent contact with my close friends! Whether through calls, meeting up in person to hang out, or exchanging text and voice messages to let them know I'm thinking of them, I find these friends as people who bring constant value into my life. Because I identify as a student of life, I find it easiest to converse with equally introspective friends. Staying in constant contact with these friends allows me to have a forum and outlet to exchange ideas we've been learning about! If I'm struggling with something personal or professional, I can seek advice and support from my close friends. If they're going through a tough time, I want to be a resource for them.

Best Friends or Chosen Family

Best friends or chosen family have developed the highest level of trust with you. You disclose your dreams, struggles, and fears with them. You have many common interests, and communication is fluid due to mutual honesty, loyalty, and respect.

In my case, these are the friends I would cry in front of. I would let them read my journal diaries because there is nothing to hide. I could count on them to lend me a couch to sleep last minute if I needed it. While this may not be true for you, my chosen family are friends who require less maintenance than close friends because our bond is as strong as blood. After a year or more of falling out of touch, I can catch up with these friends and reconnect instantaneously as if that time gap didn't exist. These are the friendships that make me feel the most at home.

HOW TO DEEPEN YOUR FRIENDSHIPS

Generally speaking, most friendships progress linearly and step-by-step through these stages, but the timeline for each unique friendship can vary drastically. Sometimes, you hit the jackpot and meet your soul sister or brother, going from stranger directly to chosen family and progressing through the four stages in one conversation. Others never move past the stranger and acquaintance phase, and that's okay! We want to build real and lasting friendships, which means you can't focus your energy on everyone. But also stay open-minded to the possibility of change. A friend you met in school who was not very close could reconnect with you later in life and become your best friend in adulthood. Life is full of surprises like this, so you just never know!

How Many Friendships Can You Reasonably Maintain

As you're starting this journey, you might get pretty excited at the possibility of all the new friendships you can make. But keep in mind how many friendships you can reasonably maintain given the following:

1. Your communication style
2. Your social battery
3. Your work style and lifestyle

4. How much effort (time) it'll take to
   preserve different friendships

Notice how in the 4 stages of friendship above, we didn't detail exactly how many friends you can have in each step. That's because, depending on your social capacity and circumstances, it may be easier or more challenging for you to manage a certain number of best friends versus close friends versus peer friends.

Life is a numbers game. The more conversations you have, the more likely you'll have good conversations. The more strangers/acquaintances you meet, the more choices you have for developing life-giving friendships.

Now that we understand your relationships' progression, let's look at how we can deepen them!

Give People a Few Chances to Warm Up to You

If, after the first impression, the conversation wasn't extraordinary but wasn't bad, don't give up on the potential budding friendship! I've found that some of my closest relationships developed over 3-10 hangouts, depending on how quickly I could become vulnerable with said friend. Sometimes the first 1-2 encounters are for understanding each other's comfort level in humor, interests, and conversation topics. Don't miss a potentially beautiful friendship because your values or interests don't match perfectly.

"Echo chamber" is a term used to describe a closed-loop social environment where a person's beliefs and opinions are resonated back to them, creating confirmation biases and eliminating possibilities of alternative perspectives. The danger of echo chambers is that they develop close-minded individuals, generating social polarization and extremism, leading to dissent and even wars (Roberts, 2019).

To actively combat this, we must educate ourselves on the full breadth of experiences and perspectives life offers by seeking collaborative conversations. So long as your values don't clash too drastically, developing deep friendships with those who appear quite different from us is possible!

Stay in Touch

Understand your friend's communication style. Do they prefer texting, voice notes, or video/voice calls? Are they someone who likes to hear from you daily, or do they not mind if you write to them once a year? Like the five love languages, understanding their expectations for staying in touch versus your own can help avoid any misunderstandings.

I'm pretty bad at responding to text messages, so I confess this to all my friends up front. For this reason, we intentionally plan more in-person hangouts, video calls, and other meaningful ways to stay in touch.

One of my favorite friendships developed organically from an online interaction where I contacted a fellow creative based in Chicago via social media. Coincidentally, I had planned a trip to Chicago a few weeks before, and one day, I randomly realized there was an opportunity to meet a new friend! So I asked if he would be open to meeting up for coffee! He said yes, and we spent hours bonding over our creative processes, taking photos while exploring the streets together, giving each other feedback on current projects over lunch, and then ending with a mini photoshoot at a cafe. Then, as we said goodbye with the genuine possibility of never spending time together in person again, he suggested we try a weekly call to keep us creatively accountable. As someone continuously seeking ways to add more art into my life, I thought this was a splendid idea! Despite busy travel schedules, full-time adulting, and juggling passion projects, we've kept up with these semi-weekly calls over the past two years. Our conversations have slowly morphed from being solely about creativity to incorporating spirituality and life purpose. Had he not suggested that we keep in touch over weekly calls as we were parting ways, our acquaintanceship wouldn't have blossomed into one of my closest friendships.

Keep the Vulnerability Going

You can practice vulnerability even outside of the actual face-to-face conversations. If someone asks you, "How's it going?" via text message, communicate how you truly feel instead of answering with the default "good." If you're struggling or suffering, share it. If possible, paint it in a hopeful light. For example, "I've been going through a rough week, but maybe next week will be better." This is not to downplay anything you may be working through or struggling with, but rather, another act of practicing optimism to support your overall mental health.

We covered asking for help and advice to keep a conversation flowing, but seeking support can also be done outside of in-person discussions. When you ask others for help, it makes others feel needed and competent, which is a feeling everyone loves. In the research of Aditi Shrikant, a psychologist and author, she found that people tend to underestimate how much others want to help. Both strangers and friends have more of a desire for you to ask them for help than you may realize (Shrikant, 2022).

Asking for help can look like giving and receiving favors. This is great for those whose love language is *acts of service*. These favors can look like anything from asking for a ride to the airport to offering to pick up groceries for them when they're sick. You can pet sit for your friends or ask them to watch your dog when you go on vacation. Just remember not to ask for a favor you wouldn't be willing to return.

Create Shared Experiences

Creating positive shared experiences is just as important as having deep conversations. Why? It generates a sense of belonging which helps with building trust and intimacy. Shared experiences, no matter how small, create shared memories that help you relate with each other by helping us become aware of our own and others' emotions. This, in turn, enables us to develop our EQ and empathy.

By bolstering *positive experiences*, we also rewire our brains to expect and look for more favorable situations. Positive experiences shared in relationships have been shown through several studies to improve your physical health (The Value of Shared Experiences | Nurse Next Door, 2019).

How to Create Shared Experiences

Below I will provide some ideas for experiences you can share with your loved ones, but the best list would be one you collaboratively create with your friends. You can approach your friend by saying, "I read this fun idea to try in a book, and I wonder if you'd be interested in trying it out with me! We will create a list of interests, hobbies, or activities we enjoy, then come together to compare and see if anything overlaps!"

Here are some possible positive shared experiences you can have with your friends!

- Joining events around town
- Attending fitness classes
- Going hiking, kayaking, camping, or rock climbing
- Asking for a lesson on a skill you want to learn from your friend (or even offering to teach a skill they're interested in)
- Playing board or card games
- Doing arts and crafts together
- Visiting a museum or park

- Cooking and sharing a meal
- Studying or coworking together!

Even if you're not studying the same subjects or working on the same team at work, this is an easy way to hang out with your pals. The idea is to meet up to get work done and use each other as accountability. These can sometimes get distracting, so set expectations upfront about how much studying or work you need to complete and plan your chatting around this.

This works great between my personal group of friends because it allows us to hang out more frequently on a casual basis. During these coworking sessions, we catch up on life and sometimes serendipitously generate ideas for future hangouts!

QUALITIES OF HEALTHY FRIENDS

As you are developing your friendships, make sure to keep note of these qualities of healthy relationships top of mind. If you find that your relationships are straying from these markers, try to address them by practicing vulnerability and bringing them up with the person in question.

Encourages New Friendships

If you're in a relationship with someone who gets jealous when you spend time with others, talks bad about other people, or discourages you from developing new friendships, you should take a step back from this friendship. Most likely, you are dealing with someone with few friends, and you're one of the only people filling up their social needs cup.

This kind of person tends to bring about codependency in a relationship. They want you to need them just as much as they need you. So, they try and cut off any new connections you may make, claiming your new work friend is annoying or doesn't get their vibe.

I had a friend like this in high school. I remember telling someone else: "Being friends with this person is like having a possessive boyfriend you can't break up with because you're already friends."

In the end, she resorted to bullying and lies to try and keep me all to herself. She'd tell me how terrible I was for not spending enough time with her, how bad of a friend I was because I couldn't come over, and how if I cared about her, I would prove it.

A healthy friend knows just how valuable you are to this world. They understand that they don't own your time and can't meet all your needs. They make new friends and want you to do the same!

Holds Authenticity

Have you ever been around someone who wants to make you hide? Maybe they make fun of you for something silly you said, or they're so judgmental of others you worry about what they might say about you when you're not around.

I once went on a boating trip with several friends from my workplace. We rented a cabin by a lake and spent the entire week playing cards, boating, and having fun on the beach. It was lovely.

The only problem was that I had one friend who loved to party. If you didn't have a drink in your hand, she'd get you one. Every night she wanted everyone to take shots with her. I found myself consoling one of my underage friends who had come with us that she didn't have to drink anything just because Zoe said she should.

There isn't anything wrong with drinking; I love to drink socially. But I'm someone who gets exceptionally nauseous if I have too much. I found myself drinking one can of beer, then running to the bathroom with the empty can every half hour to fill it with water. That way, if Zoe came my way and picked up my drink to see how much progress I had made, it seemed like I was still drinking beer.

You don't want a circle of friends to hide from.

Keeping up with appearances to impress other people is exhausting. A high-quality friend is someone with whom you can be totally yourself around.

Every person on earth has flaws that they need to work on. My hope for you is that you meet the kind of people who can eventually see every shortcoming you possess and still love you.

These types of friends exist. You just have to find them.

Creates Mutual Respect

Mutual respect is one of the essential pillars of a healthy relationship. Of course, everyone acts disrespectfully at some point in life, whether on accident or on purpose. You don't need a perfect friend in this area. You just need someone who is mature enough to listen to you wholeheartedly and to treat you well even if they disagree with you. That way, negative feelings don't develop into passive aggression.

These friends will let you know if you say something that steps on their toes. Likewise, if they do something that bothers you, you know you can go to them and have an honest, open conversation about it. They won't blow up, get defensive, or harass you with a list of ways you've failed them. They'll listen intently and change their behavior, just like you do for them when they come to you with something in their heart.

A person who encourages mutual respect might look like: someone who asks you about your feelings and honestly shares their own, someone who doesn't gossip about others behind their back but goes to talk it out with the person who hurt them, and someone who, when you approach them with a challenging and uncomfortable topic, is all ears.

Their friendship with you is based on something more than always having the same opinion. You enjoy each other's company, regardless of your differences.

High-Quality, Low-Maintenance

I have a great friend from college, Rachel, who I absolutely adore. She's funny, authentic, and simply easy to talk to. After we graduated, I started a new job, and she went to graduate school. She was paying for her tuition with a research assistantship. Suddenly, we found ourselves in a situation where we didn't have much time to talk to each other. We used to get dinner every week, but now we call maybe every eight months.

You would think our connection would fade with

so many miles between us and so much time between calls. But the opposite is true! Every phone call, we talk about all the major events in our lives and how we've been these last few months. Then, Rachel will always say, "And how are you really doing, emotionally and spiritually?"

We'll then discuss what's on our hearts. She called just yesterday, and I told her I had taken on a second job and was already feeling burnt out and worried I had inherited my parents' addiction to work. She told me about her family and some things I don't wish to share here. She ended the conversation with: "I haven't really had a chance to process this with anyone yet, and it's nice to get it all off my chest."

I don't know when I'll be able to see Rachel face-to-face again. But I know that whenever I call her, she'll eventually return it, and we'll sit around for the evening, both of us sipping on wine or eating our dinners, miles and miles apart.

If you can find a friend who can provide you with all the other qualities of healthy friendships mentioned here while remaining low-maintenance, know that friendship is a real blessing.

Encourages You to Adapt

The reason that I decided to start swing dancing

is that I had a friend who, almost every weekend, invited me to go with him. Initially, I thought learning to dance at a bar would be publicly humiliating. I'm *so* clumsy, and I didn't want to go display these things to the whole world.

So, my friend told me that he could show me some moves at his apartment. Afterward, we would go to the bar. Finally, I said yes just to humor him. In a shocking turn of events, I had a great time! Turns out, swing dancing isn't so hard, and everyone at the bar was learning at a different level.

Healthy friends will encourage you to grow, including in social situations you're uncomfortable with. They're patient, understanding, and willing to help transition you into these new scenarios rather than dropping you into cold water.

Makes You Feel Supported and Loved

One of the most harrowing experiences of my life was when my little brother, David, was paralyzed from the waist down in a car accident that nearly took his life. I dropped out of college, lived with him through his rehabilitation, and turned into a sad, empty shell of the person I once was.

I had regressed to my high school self: exhausted, sad for no reason, and riddled with grief. I knew I wasn't as funny as I used to be, and somehow, I felt slower, like maybe all my smarts had been sucked out of my brain by these difficult circumstances.

My friends stopped talking to me because they didn't know what to say. I had people tell me over and over that they missed the *old* me: the happy, cheery, and funny person I was before this event. I even had one friend call me to say that she didn't want to be friends with me at all anymore. I was just an echo of my old self; she didn't want to put up with the person I had become.

I will always remember a dinner I had with my good friend, Sherry. We have been friends since the fifth grade, and we graduated high school and went to college together. I was sitting in the cafeteria, crying into my chicken noodle soup.

"I just feel sad. I haven't been this sad since high school—everyone keeps saying they miss having the old me around. I miss *being* the old me."

My friend Sherry grabbed my hand and said, "You know, I loved high school you. I loved you before the car accident, and I love you now. I don't care how you are—I'm gonna love you until we're dead."

This moment, which Sherry perhaps doesn't even remember, was one of the things that got me through that difficult period of life. Yes, I went through some changes, and I lost some friends. But the ones who stuck around ended up being the biggest blessings in my life.

I've made all kinds of new friends that didn't even know the person I was before my little brother's car accident. I cherish them deeply. But the ones who stuck around, even as I became a less pleasant presence in their life, mean something special to me.

If you find yourself in a similar situation where your life changes drastically and you grow into a different person, feel free to grieve the friends you lose along the way. But don't let that grief stop you from being grateful for the friends who stay. Those are the real gems—the friendships that last.

In retrospect, I'm thankful that some people faded out of my life during that time. They were great blessings for a period, but it was good that they walked away when they no longer desired to be my friend. That freed up my time to make better friendships with folks who delighted in the person I truly was.

Your friends ought to make you feel loved and supported. If somebody doesn't support you the way you need them to, don't chase them down and tell them how they should be acting. But it is your responsibility to develop your community of people who can support and love you in the way you need.

Brings Joy To Your Life

One of the most underrated things you can do for your mental health, self-esteem, and well-being is to have fun! You need some of your relationships to be folks who bring joy and playfulness into your life.

There are so many shades of fun, and your friends can help you experience many of them. I know some people who love bar trivia and go out every Wednesday to win trivia contests. I love to dance and go out with a group every Saturday to hone these skills.

Watching my little brother, Dontavious, play football is one of the most enjoyable moments in my life. David, his wife, Natalie, and I all road trip together to watch him on Friday nights. I know nothing about football, but I know Dontavious is good at it. We all wear T-shirts with his face on them, and afterward, we go back to my dad's house and sit around eating jalapeno poppers and drinking together.

You would think someone who knows nothing about sports would not have a great time at a football game. But my relationship with my family and the fun I get to have with them make it so worth it.

Whatever your definition is of fun, you need people in your life who can enjoy it with you. Maybe that's board games, video games, book clubs, or sitting around on the back porch, drinking beer and chatting about the meaning of life. This will also hold you accountable to enjoy this precious life you live!

Helps You Draw Healthy Boundaries

A good friend will also help you develop the skill set of being assertive. Why? Because they care about you! Sometimes, as an introvert, I struggle to stand up for myself. People will act in ways that hurt or disrespect me, and instead of saying something about it to resolve the issue, I'll fall into silence and carry this burden around.

The other day, I told one of my work friends that my lead had acted somewhat inappropriately. A new project had to be done, and he gave it to one of his friends in the department with less education and experience than I had. While I disagreed with the decision, I told my friend I didn't want to stir up any trouble.

"Well, STIR UP THE TROUBLE!" she interrupted me, "That bozo needs to give these projects to qualified people!"

She then told me how I wasn't just helping myself by standing up for what was right, I was helping the whole department. Did I want this person to always get every project forever? Or did I want to help the company by holding my lead accountable for his actions? This encouraged me to have a challenging and scary discussion with my lead.

It's hard to set boundaries with people, but it's much easier when you have friends who encourage you to. Having someone in your life who makes it clear that they want you to be comfortable in your friendships and your life is an invaluable asset.

Balances "Me" Time vs. Social Time

Healthy relationships honor the fact that different people have different needs. Some folks are recharged by being alone; others by being around people! As an introvert, it's not that you don't like being around others, but when you need rest, you do so by having time to yourself.

You want to be in a respectful friendship that honors your needs. If you need a substantial amount of time alone, find someone with a big social circle who doesn't always come to you when they need to chat! If you have friends who recharge by being around others, encourage them to build a large social circle so someone's always available to spend time with them.

Makes You Feel Safe

The most crucial quality in a friend is that they make you feel safe. You know they won't make fun of you for feeling your feelings, being who you are, or your goofy dance moves at the club. You can say what comes into your mind without fear of judgment or abandonment.

I tend to think of my friends Sherry and Rachel as I write these words. These are the people who I can call when I have a burden on my heart.

It does not matter what topic we discuss or what faux pas we may commit. We support and love each other at every turn.

Just this past New Year's, Sherry and I had a party with friends. We discussed washing clothes you buy at the store before you wear them, which I found to be a much more controversial topic than I expected.

Sherry shared she didn't wash her clothes, and everyone else was ganging up on her. They were saying things like: "That's totally disgusting!" And: "I could never imagine doing that!"

I was tempted to keep quiet because I never wash the clothes I buy at the store, either. I thought I'd be especially ridiculed, given that I shop exclusively at thrift stores most of the time. I have too many other things to worry about; I can't gather the energy to wash new clothes. I didn't want the rest of the party to focus on discussing how disgusting I was. But I could tell Sherry was feeling singled out and uncomfortable.

"I just don't have the time to live my life in fear!" I said. "I have much better things to do than to wash my *brand-new clothes!* I don't even have time to think about who might have tried them on at the store!"

Sherry smiled with relief. "Exactly!"

It was small, but it changed the tone of the discussion. Suddenly, the guests weren't singling out Sherry for an odd habit. We began debating the merits of the practice in general.

My friendship with Rachel also makes me feel safe because she is genuine. Rachel will be the first person to tell you that her personality can be off-putting. How do I know this? She told me the first week I met her.

"Being friends with me is like eating mushrooms. I'm an acquired taste."

This phrase made me laugh and laugh. And I soon understood where she was coming from. Rachel can be intense. She doesn't keep her opinions to herself. If you don't have the right mindset when you talk with her, you might be prone to getting your feelings hurt just because of her blunt way of communicating.

Her birthday rolled around, and on her card, I wrote, "I think I have acquired this taste." She later asked me to dinner, and we became close, and the rest is history.

Feeling safe doesn't always necessarily mean agreeing with each other, but you always have each other's back. The friends who make you feel safe will help you to embrace all the quirks that make you human and unique!

CHAPTER 8
CONFLICTS AND LETTING GO

What do you do in situations where you encounter tension? Encountering conflicts and struggles are a natural part of developing relationships. Instead of shying away from them and allowing them to ruin your life, managing and resolving disputes effectively can minimize drama and enhance your sense of self and belonging!

AVOIDING CONFLICT

In some cases, the best solution is to avoid instigating conflict altogether. This works best in new and developing relationships (those in the earlier stages of friendship) as these people have yet to earn your trust and time to be worth the effort needed for severe intervention. If you're employing the strategies of FLOW, you should naturally avoid misunderstandings by staying open-minded and curious via active listening and optimism. But here are some other details to keep in mind!

Taboo Topics

Taboo topics usually are political or social issues rooted in painful, often explosive, and polarizing emotions for people. What's considered taboo depends on the time in history you're living in, someone's generation, a person's personality and beliefs, and the setting where you're discussing these topics. Current taboo topics include abortion, gossip, cannibalism, death and suicide, politics, money and salaries, profanity, religion, weight, and age.

What do you do when taboo topics come up? If you feel comfortable proceeding with the topic, you can listen and learn. And if not, change the subject! You can be vulnerable and say, "I'm uncomfortable talking about this. Can we talk about something else?" Or, more subtly, "Interesting... you know what else is interesting?" and change the topic yourself.

Note that these topics are best avoided early on in a new friendship, but if throughout collaborative conversations, these topics come up and both you and your conversation partner are comfortable with discussing them in a mature and encouraging nature, examining complex issues like these can be an act of vulnerability and deepen your relationship.

People to Avoid

Avoid those who don't respect you. There's no reason to try to make these friendships work. Maybe in the future, something will change, and they may become more respectful. If it happens, great! You can try to give them a second chance. If it doesn't, let it go.

Avoid people who don't know how to carry on a conversation. Suppose you have a lukewarm conversation, but your conversation partner just doesn't know how to ask questions to help carry the conversation forward. This indicates that they're not one to take the initiative or perhaps not collaborative. If so, trying to develop a friendship with them could mean you'll have to carry the brunt of starting conversations and planning hangouts. If you find yourself in such circumstances, know that making these relationships work is not your job. Conversations and connections require collective effort!

Trust Your Gut

If something feels off during a conversation or interaction, your intuition is telling you to leave! Instead of waiting to see what happens next, politely exit and distance yourself. This could happen with strangers or even people you already know. Either way, it is easier to remove yourself than to accidentally develop a toxic relationship that may be harder to exit in the future.

Ideas for exiting a conversation in an emergency:

- Ask for directions to the restroom!
- Say you have an immediate obligation to attend to (this could be a made-up task or a made-up friend who is "waiting to meet with you")!

Pro tip: Register for a Google Voice number so if someone asks for your number and won't leave you unless you text them, you can give a false "real" number.

CONFLICT RESOLUTION

Conflict resolution is an art of vulnerability because it requires recognizing and admitting that there is a problem, then having the courage to address it. It often feels even more involved when it concerns someone we care about deeply. However, instead of avoiding the issue out of fear, you can use the dispute to learn more about each other and grow closer by facing the issue together. Yes, *TOGETHER*, because conflicts are not you versus the other person in question. Rather, conflicts are actually you *AND* the other person versus the problem. Enter with this mindset and encourage the other person to view the problem with this perspective as well.

Types of Conflict

Before examining some practical and research-based steps to resolve conflict, we'll review the challenges you may face.

Information Conflict

An information conflict arises when you and someone you have a relationship with have different data or stories you're working off of (*11.3: Four Major Types of Conflict* | 2022).

I vividly remember from middle school sending a text that I felt was noninflammatory. My friend blew up the next day, and we texted back and forth for almost the entire weekend over this one misunderstanding. She was hurt and wouldn't tell me why, and I had no idea where her anger was coming from. After scrolling back in our texts, I realized I had forgotten one comma, which changed the meaning and tone of the entire message. An information conflict can be solved both with active listening and optimism. More on that in a minute.

Values Conflict

A values conflict arises when one party perceives the other party to have incompatible values (Times & Times, 2023). These conflicts can often be triggered by taboo subjects such as politics and religion.

Just because you and a friend may have a values conflict doesn't mean you should throw out the entire relationship. Some of my best friends think differently about politics and religion, and I enjoy debating with them! As long as you and your friend know how to communicate healthily and respectfully, having conflicting values is not a deal-breaker for friendships.

Trust Conflict

A trust conflict appears when one person thinks that the other is acting maliciously toward them (Vilendrer, 2014). Trust conflicts are the most painful because one party believes the other has it out for them.

I experienced this kind of conflict at the beginning of the school year. My principal was furious with me for not submitting my timesheet on time. She emailed me several emails about how I had missed and ignored her deadline and then texted me that I needed to get it in as soon as possible. I was on vacation with my extended family, so I ignored emails and texts until I got home. I was hurt because I had turned in my timesheet by the deadline. I felt like maybe my principal had it out for me because she knew I was leaving at the end of the year. I moped around my house and told my family how unfair my boss was, how irritating and disrespectful her behavior was, and how excited I was to leave my current school.

Later, a colleague texted me, saying the same thing had happened to her. We decided that our principal must have lost the time sheets and that she didn't really have it out for us. She was lashing out from frustration. Even though her anger isn't an excuse for her behavior, at least I could go into this year without fear that my boss was looking for reasons to undermine me.

Structural Conflicts

Structural conflicts occur from people acting disrespectfully because of a lack of resources (Rose, 2022). This conflict will often happen between siblings. When my little brother was younger, he would steal all the desserts from our pantry and hide them in our room. My other siblings would become irate, and we would go ravaging through his stuff in search of Oreos.

As an adult, this conflict can look like hiding information. For example, my coworker and I want to leave our current place of work, and I see an excellent listing for better money at a different school. When my coworker texted me later to ask me to send her the link to the job application, I hesitated and was tempted to ignore her text, so I'd be more likely to get the job. But after some thought, I decided that my relationships mean more to me than getting away from my current situation. So I sent her the application. Neither of us got the job, but I'm happy to know that my friendship with my coworker means more to me than a pay raise.

If I had refused to send her the job listing, that would have hurt our relationship, and this conflict would have been a good example of a structural conflict.

HOW TO RESOLVE CONFLICTS

If active listening and optimism have yet to help with the conflicts described above, try the following strategies.

If You're Wrong, Admit It!

This can be hard for some people. It hurts the ego to have to admit that you were wrong. But some relationships are not worth losing over your pride. This simple act of vulnerability and respect for the other person will show your sincerity and commitment to resolving the issue and help remove blockers from collaborative conversation. Your confession can encourage the other person to be more flexible and open-minded, allowing you two to reach a compromise or resolution faster.

Ask Questions (Don't Give Advice)

Even when giving advice, try to lead the other person to the correct answer instead of ordering them around. If you tell them everything they're doing wrong, they'll walk away wounded and irritated. Help them come to more satisfactory decisions by asking better questions!

Instead of saying, "Well, you should take your mom up on her offer for the two of you to go to therapy. Nothing will ever get better unless you guys address your issues."

Try asking, "Do you want a future relationship with your mom? Do you think you can take steps to accomplish that without therapy?"

This takes practice to learn, especially if you tend to be solution and action-oriented. I once had a friend who always complained about being single! Every time, I would advise the same thing.

"Well, why don't you get on a dating app?! That's where people meet these days; I don't think anything's going to happen unless you take steps to solve this problem!"

At the time, I was approaching my friend with sympathy instead of empathy. I wasn't thinking about how hard it must have been to move to a new city for her job and start over, to put hours of work into a career when at the end of the day, she just wanted to be a stay-at-home mom. Instead, I thought about how I would handle the situation if I was in her shoes.

She wasn't ready for that step right then, which wasn't her fault! It would have been so much better for me to take a step back and ask her how she might accomplish her goals instead of me ordering my will on the issue.

You can't make people do what you think they should do. At the end of the day, it's their life. So, if you want to help them, ask them about their options and why they're making the decisions they're making! You'll increase your empathy for your friend and potentially guide them to a better solution for themself.

I later apologized to my friend for pushing her hard to join a dating app. I could tell I had upset her. She told me she wasn't ready and wanted to be healthier before dating anyone. This was a wise choice on her part. If I had just asked the right questions and listened actively, I would have understood where she was coming from.

Here's another example of using active listening and probing questions to establish expectations and avoid conflicts. If your roommate is too messy and it's driving you insane, don't tell them that they're gross for living into their everyday habits. Just ask what they think is a reasonable tidiness around the house. Then, you can share your own opinion on this issue respectfully. If you two have different views about how clean the house should be, ask something like:

"What would be a good compromise so that the

kitchen doesn't require too much work but could satisfy both of us?"

Note that by asking for their opinion, you're not directing how the compromise should play out.

SETTING HEALTHY BOUNDARIES

Boundaries are any limits you place in your life. Healthy boundaries communicate with yourself and others what you will and will not tolerate. For example, if you don't put boundaries on your work hours, then ambition and love for money will run your life. Suppose you don't put limits on your social life. In that case, you'll sacrifice the quality of your time with your community by showing up for all hangouts and not being mentally there (instead of showing up for only some meetups and being totally present). If you don't put boundaries on hobbies, it might consume you and financially cost you by making you buy things to feed them. Therefore, setting limits and boundaries is essential to your well-being, and doing so will create peace in your life.

I used to be someone who had very poor boundaries. If you needed help with something, I was the gal to ask. On top of taking care of my brothers, I was constantly playing therapist to all of my friends. It was no wonder that I was always exhausted and held a silent bitterness for most people in my life, all because I didn't know how to say "no" when they asked me to do something.

Once I got to college, I read a book on boundaries, which changed my life. I realized it wasn't everyone else's fault for asking me for help all the time; it was my fault for not knowing how to refuse to help people when I needed to rest!

Set and communicate your boundaries early in your relationship to avoid one-sided conflicts such as resentment. It's scary and requires vulnerability because sometimes we fall into the trap that people will only love us if we always say yes. We think this of our families, bosses, and friends. But nothing could be further from the truth! If the people in your life stop loving you based on what you can and can't do for them, are they worth having around?

As a middle school teacher, I see this all the time. Most of my coworkers believe that to be an effective teacher, you must take work home. They teach extra classes, train new employees, and live in terror of failing our principal.

When my boss asked me to train a new teacher, I had to stop by her office and let her know that I would not be performing tasks that had nothing to do with my job. I told her that I would consider this offer if she trained me to be a teacher coach and then paid me as one. A lot of my coworkers thought I was crazy. After all, everyone knew I was leaving this middle school and needed letters of recommendation for a new job. But I decided that I don't really care if my principal lets my new boss know that I only do work that I'm paid for. I'd rather be hired by someone who expects me to work with excellence but with firm boundaries instead of expecting me to make their school my whole life.

Have these boundaries hurt my work? Absolutely not. I'm a much kinder teacher because I come into school well-rested and brimming with other experiences that bolster my mood.

People with healthy boundaries aren't prone to being taken advantage of, don't do things they don't really want to do, and only take on tasks they can handle. They tend to have a strong sense of identity and are not guilty of saying no to people. Conversely, those with unhealthy boundaries give too much time to others, feel guilty over saying no, and have lower self-esteem (Hailey, 2022).

Think of and Name Your Limits

One great tactic for setting boundaries is deciding what they are! Don't wait until you're at the end of your rope and exhausted to say, "Wow, maybe I need a little bit more alone time." Try to decide these things beforehand. That way, when someone asks you to go over your limits, you've already decided you can't. If you name your limits ahead, you'll be able to name them to others as well.

Try and visualize what may cross a boundary, whether it's your parents asking you to pick up your little brother from the airport on a workday or a friend insisting you spend the weekend with them. Then, decide what you might say in response.

"Oh, I totally would, but I already have plans!" These plans might look like sitting on your couch with a glass of wine, watching The Office. Your mom and dad don't have to know that.

Or you can just say that you need some rest, "Oh man, I totally would, but I think I need to introvert it up this weekend."

Or naming the fact that you can only be spoken to in a certain way, "Let's continue this conversation when we can both be respectful. I'm gonna leave and let you cool off for a while."

Have a line for when your boss asks you to work overtime, "Shoot, I would, but I actually have a policy where I don't take work home."

Ensure you have visualized how you want to communicate any boundary you need in your life.

Doing so will be extremely helpful when you inevitably have to set them (Hailey, 2022).

Openly Communicate Your Boundaries!

People can't read minds. If you're not up for something, it's your job to say so! Here are some boundaries you can consider setting to protect your mental health.

Time

You can set time boundaries for just about anything. "I'll be there, but only for an hour!" or "Shoot me a text if you're gonna be late!" lets the people around you know that your time has limits (*What Are Time Boundaries and How to Set Them Up?*, 2022). This is especially important for friends who tend to get caught up in conversations or hangouts past when they intend to.

I confess I tend to let time slide by while trying to get out of a conversation. The other day, a coworker stopped by my desk to chat. She talked so long, complaining about everything from her job to her sister-in-law, that I finally got up and said I needed to go to the bathroom to end the conversation! This could have been easily avoided if, at some point early on in our chat, I had something like, "I got a lot of work, so I can only chat for a few minutes." Communicating your time boundaries ahead of time helps to keep your and your friend's expectations in sync.

Energy

You have a responsibility to ensure you use your energy well. How will you perform well at your job if you constantly offer your time for other people's jobs? How can you enjoy your life if you're exhausted from overcommitting to other people's priorities?

When protecting your energy, you can say, "I don't have the energy to help you with _____ today." Even if you feel selfish for saying so, sometimes, we just don't have the energy to help others, which is totally okay!

This boundary goes for your emotional energy as well. Maybe you spent all night caring for your sick kid at home. Coming into work the next day to have your coworker cry about their spouse might be too much. It's good to say, "I am so sorry that you're going through these things, but I just don't have the emotional capacity to be a listening ear today."

If you don't guard your energy, people will learn that you're always up to say yes, and then you'll be the first person they go to when they have a burden on their hearts or a task they need help with. It's lovely to help others! But being always available to help is a surefire way of always being asked and never having time for our needs.

Conversational

Sometimes, you just have to let people know what is and is not okay to say in front of you (*When Conversation Boundaries Are Crossed*, n.d.). Maybe it's a topic that reminds you of a traumatic event. Perhaps it's something that makes you feel uncomfortable. Whatever it is, it's okay for you to say, "I don't really want to talk about this right now." You can also use this sentence to deter unwelcome or rude jokes. "I don't really find those kinds of comments funny."

Conversational boundaries can protect your mind in a way other limits can't. If someone is being pushy about their unwelcome opinion, it is healthy for you to say, "I appreciate and respect your right to that opinion, but please don't force it on me!" Doing so respects your conversation partner by being honest and open with them about how you feel. It's also self-respecting because you safeguard your mind and emotions.

Physical

Physical boundaries are essential to any relationship. Whether romantic or platonic, sometimes you don't want other people's hands on certain body parts. Be ready to say, "It makes me uncomfortable when you touch _____. If you keep doing so, I will have to leave." Give your children these words to know they can flee uncomfortable or dangerous situations. Give yourself these words to guard your physical being to be comfortable. If someone can't respect your physical boundaries, then it may be time to reconsider this person's place in your life (Mindbodygreen, 2022).

Physical boundaries don't just apply to your body. They apply to your possessions as well!

If someone borrows your mug without asking, don't silently resent them for it, passive-aggressively suggest it was your *go-to* or *favorite* mug, or start hiding your things around your room. Tell the person who borrowed it you would prefer it if they asked! It's your stuff, after all.

INITIATING A DIFFICULT CONVERSATION

Whether it's a confrontation of values, crossing a boundary or setting one, or addressing a recurring issue, you will likely have to practice conflict resolution across your relationships. So, here are some helpful sentence starters to keep in your back pocket!

Asking to Talk and Setting Your Intentions

Sometimes, it's good to just be able to define your friendship, set your intentions, or let friends know where you stand on a particular issue. These sentence starters can look like this: "I was hoping to talk to you about ____." Or "I wish to understand your point of view better so that _____."

Sharing Your Feelings

This is a great one for when someone hurts your feelings. I am one of the most sensitive people I know, so I use this line left and right to get through my day without letting lies take root in my heart!

If someone says or does something hurtful, you can say: "The story I'm creating in my head when you said/did that is that _____." By framing the issue from this point of view, you're acknowledging that whatever they did or said may not have been intentional or that you're not directly blaming them for your reaction.

When You Need More Time to Think About an Issue

If something abruptly occurs and opens a sudden, deep emotional wound, you might naturally over-react out of fear, anger, sadness, or confusion. Please take a deep breath and know you don't need to resolve it immediately. It's better to gather your thoughts and gain some perspective before making your case.

Here, you can say, "I would love to reflect a bit more on the situation before we discuss it. Do you have time tomorrow to address this?"

Following Up On a Conversation

If you started a conversation that ended without closure, you might have to suggest continuing it. "Yesterday, we talked about___, and I would like to know what your thoughts are on it now."

Letting a situation sit for a day (or some time) can be helpful if both parties are mature and reflective. They can more clearly reflect on the issue alone, come to more concrete conclusions about where they stand, and can return later to discuss a conflict from a more rational and potentially less-emotional outset.

Recurring Issues

You want to be careful with your tone when you bring up recurring issues. Approach the problem with a smile and genuine curiosity to understand the root of *why* this keeps happening. It could come off as accusing if you ask too abruptly or assertively.

Try, "I've noticed that _____. I would love to better understand why ____ so we can work/live better together."

> **Pro tip:** You can soften the impact of bringing up a conflict point by highlighting your own capacity to make mistakes. This humanizes you and signals that you're not perfect, either.

I have personally used the following script to strengthen my closest relationships.

"There's been something on my mind, and I wanted to bring it up with you because I really care about our friendship and want to understand you and us better. Remember when _____? The story I created in my head when that happened is that _____. I know I'm not perfect, and I make mistakes. And I want to ensure I'm not mistaken by misinterpreting the events or your intentions."

EXPECTATIONS (WHY YOU NEED THEM)

Expectations are like self-fulfilling prophecies that can literally bend reality. When people believe a particular medicine or practice will heal them, their body releases the hormones they need to feel less pain under what is known as the placebo effect. Patients administered dummy pills under the pretense that these drugs had actual medical efficacy have been shown to cure their conditions such as fatigue, pain, or nausea (Harvard Health, 2021).

You can use your expectations to change your social circumstances as well! A 1960s study showed that when teachers were told that one class had higher performers than the other, they treated who they thought to be high performers as such. In contrast, they treated the other class normally. By the end of the year, the "high-performing" class was doing much better than the other one. The twist? The classes started the year at the same level (Washington, 2019).

Thus, you can use expectations to create the best outcomes for your friendships and relationships. For example, in conflict situations, you can trust and expect that the person will receive the message and want to collaborate with you to find a solution and preserve the friendship!

But be careful. You can also use expectations to end friendships. If you expect to be betrayed by someone (whether you have evidence or not), you're less likely to trust them and stay guarded during conversations, leading to the eventual death of a friendship.

For this reason, we practice optimism and positivity. Our minds set our expectations, which ultimately change our realities.

On Failure and Letting Go

In building relationships, "failure" can look like any of the following scenarios.

- Flat-out rejection. Someone doesn't want to hang out with you, you don't get invited to that party, or you're simply ghosted.
- Maybe you meet a compatible person, but they want to dominate your social life and ask you to isolate yourself from other friendships due to jealousy or narcissism. You realize how unhealthy this friendship is and must respectfully distance yourself from this relationship as soon as possible. You feel disappointed in yourself for

allowing this person into your life as they do not have your best interest at heart.

- You accidentally touch on a taboo topic you couldn't research and prepare for due to the unique culture and upbringing of the person you're talking with. You feel embarrassed and awkward. Maybe the situation haunts you as you keep replying it in your mind.

- You've realized that a friend you've had since elementary school feels more like a stranger than a friend. You feel it's wrong to let the friendship go because you've known each other for so long and seen each other through life, but none of your interests or values match up anymore. But you feel like it's time to move on.

You trusted that things would work out, but then they didn't. How do we cope and overcome?

Acknowledge and Accept

Whether it is outgrowing a friendship, feeling guilty about something you said or did, or dealing with rejection, it hurts. Grieving and moving on involves feeling your feelings! Don't suppress your

HOW TO TALK TO ANYONE FOR INTROVERTS

pain by pretending something isn't embarrassing. Acknowledge how much you're suffering and that it stinks. This is the first step to healing from the pain (Morin, 2015)!

Don't Take It Personally

It's easy to blame ourselves when we face rejection. But the reality of your situation is that too many factors in this world might cause you to face rejection. You think that the person doesn't like you. But more likely? They're busy! They can't keep up with the friends they have! They're too tired from working two jobs! There are too many reasons someone might dismiss you for you to blame yourself for it (*4 Strategies to Cope with Rejection* | Psychology Today, n.d.).

Remember that everyone is going through their own struggles, just as you are. There is no need to apply pressure to a friendship if your friend cannot reciprocate right now.

Accept that sometimes things don't work out with certain people, and that's ok. Not everyone will be compatible with you, and that's a fact of life.

Practice Optimism and Resilience

Recognize that one wrong word or action doesn't

have to be the end of a friendship. You can always change a situation's direction, whether by apologizing, finding a compromise, or letting go. Everyone makes mistakes, and that's normal.

Also, know that if a friendship or relationship needs to end, this doesn't mean that you no longer have any friends, nor are you incapable of making more friends in the future!

Resilience is a skill set you can learn. The more you practice optimism, the more your brain will automatically lean toward positivity. Take everything you've learned from your life lesson (failure), and do it better next time! Maybe it can't be with the same person, so it has to be with a new friend. Regardless, you always have the opportunity to try again. Just remember to speak to yourself kindly, and don't let these failures define who you are (Morin, 2015)!

CONCLUSION

I hope this book has made you smile and reminded you of how powerful and important you are. Even with a just small close knit-group of friends, you have the influence to improve the social health of everyone you connect with and enhance the quality and longevity of life for you and all your loved ones.

If you take nothing else from this book, I want you to remember…

- You have the power to change any aspect of your life. Your mind is an incredible tool that can bend reality. Start where you're comfortable and push your comfort zone little by little!

- Aim for vulnerability and authenticity! These will form the most heartwarming and life-giving connections and significantly increase your social health.

- Practice optimism and resilience. Don't give up even if you encounter failures because failing is just a part of life! They also serve as useful information for how you can improve next time!

Because you've invested the time to read this book, I've thrown in a bonus 7-Day Challenge (see the following pages) to help you immediately start taking action today! After you apply all the techniques in this book, go back to Chapter 3 and review who you have become! You may find that you'll have to revise your goals based on your improvements!

If you found this book helpful, I would be honored if you could leave a review on Amazon so that other introverts can also find this book and start upgrading their lives.

And remember, just as there are SO many people to meet and learn from, there are so many people who need to meet YOU. Thank you for existing.

XinYi Xan

BONUS: 7-DAY CHALLENGE

This concise social challenge will allow you to see your results in a week! Remember that depending on the goal you choose for the challenge, achieving the desired result may not be possible after only 7 days. However, don't be discouraged! You can then review the results and repeat the week-long challenge with either the same or a different goal! I intentionally designed the challenge to be short, so you can stay motivated without losing steam, review your results faster, and keep improving in rapid iterations. I even threw in rest days for your much-needed introvert recovery time!

DAY 1: PICK YOUR GOALS + DO SOME PREP

Pick one goal to focus on, whether starting a conversation, keeping the conversation flowing, being vulnerable, or ending conversations gracefully.

Write it down in a place you can visibly see daily. Then prepare for the upcoming week!

- Do you need to set up a meeting with someone to practice your goal? Send them a message to hang out. Do you need to prepare some questions for an event? Write some questions down. Do you need to be somewhere specific to encounter strangers to start chatting? Block out a date and time to be at this particular location this week.
- Arrange to talk to your comfort person on Day 2 (see Day 2), whether that's via a voice or video call or a physical meetup.

DAY 2: BOOST YOUR SELF-CONFIDENCE

Talk to someone you love and trust and enjoy the conversation (this must be a real-time conversation that is NOT via text). This will warm you up to talk to someone you're less comfortable with by getting you into the practice of verbal communication. I emphasize that this cannot be via text because communicating verbally differs from writing because you don't have time to deliberate or perfect your responses.

No agenda and no need to challenge yourself here. Just enjoy the conversation! Appreciate that you've already made this connection and trust you can do it again with someone else.

Is no one available? That's okay! Talk to yourself in a mirror and practice being a good best friend to yourself. It may feel funny, but the idea is to get you to verbalize so your words can flow. While facing a mirror, you can practice thinking of questions to ask someone. You can even practice speaking positively about yourself (to boost self-esteem and confidence)!

Today should leave you feeling energized for the upcoming week's challenge!

DAY 3– 5: PRACTICE, PRACTICE, PRACTICE

For these 3 days, I want you to practice as much as possible! Depending on your goal, you may only have one opportunity to practice (especially if your goal is situated around a specific event) or could be as many times as possible if you're trying to say hi to random strangers.

Regardless of how often you get to practice, reflect (preferably on paper such as a journal) a bit after each practice session to celebrate what you did well and what you want to improve on!

DAY 6: TAKE A STEP BACK AND SOCIALLY RECHARGE

You can pat yourself on your back for having marathoned something you're uncomfortable with. Do something you love solo to socially recharge! It could be making a nice cup of tea and reading your favorite book, enjoying nature alone, or setting aside time to indulge in your hobbies.

DAY 7: REFLECT

Yes, you've been reflecting after each practice session throughout the week, but here is your opportunity to step back and evaluate all the data together as a whole. Did you note any patterns? Did you make any improvements over time? Try really hard to find a win, even if it's small! After all, the sum of tiny improvements will make you stop one day and realize how far you've come!

. . .

What's Next?

- That may have felt really intense, and you need to chill! No problem! Take a break for a few days (or even a week) and return the next!
- Maybe you saw some improvements but want a lot more! Okay, so do that challenge again with the same goal!
- Maybe you saw significant improvements and were satisfied with the outcome. Amazing! Pick a new goal and keep improving.

If you need even further accountability and motivation, I offer a 12-week one-on-one personal coaching program to make your goals a reality! Interested? You can book a **free consultation** call here: https://rebrand.ly/xinyi-coaching

AUTHOR BIOS

Xinyi Xan is the author of this book and founder of Don't Be Strangers, a podcast and global community for introverts and open-minded students of life who believe that there is something to be learned from everyone. She considers having a deeper relationship with oneself the key to more profound connections with others. Xinyi wrote this book because she knows how important her readers are and believes that their conversations with others are vital to the well-being of this world.

Margaret O'Connor is a ghostwriter and middle-school English teacher. She helped to write this manuscript.

REFERENCES

4 Strategies to Cope With Rejection | Psychology Today. (n.d.). Www.psychologytoday.com. https://www.psychologytoday.com/us/blog/conquering-codependency/202106/4-strategies-cope-rejection

Brown, B. (2012). Daring Greatly: *How the Courage to Be Vulnerable Transforms the Way We live, love, parent, and Lead*. Gotham Books.

Cafarchio, P. (n.d.). *How to Make the Friends You've Always Wanted.*

Can Courage Be Taught? | Psychology Today. (n.d.). Www.psychologytoday.com. Retrieved January 29, 2023, from https://www.psychologytoday.com/us/blog/hide-and-seek/201207/can-courage-be-taught

Chapman, G. (n.d.). *What are The 5 Love Languages*? 5lovelanguages.com. https://5lovelanguages.com/learn

A Few Requirements for a Strong Friendship. (2020, October 28). One Love Foundation. https://www.joinonelove.org/learn/5-requirements-for-a-strong-friendship/

Fuchs, E., & Flügge, G. (2002). *Social stress in tree shrews*. Pharmacology Biochemistry and Behavior, 73(1), 247–258. https://doi.org/10.1016/s0091-3057(02)00795-5

Gratitude: the simple way to make your relationship better and happier | *Toucan*. (n.d.). Toucan. https://toucantogether.com/blog/gratitude-the-simple-way-to-make-your-relationship-better-and-happier

Hailey, L. (2022, April 15). *How to Set Boundaries: 5 Ways to Draw the Line Politely*. Science of People. https://www.scienceofpeople.com/how-to-set-boundaries/

Halton, M. (2022, October 16). *Humans are made to be touched — so what happens when we aren't?* ideas.ted.com. https://ideas.ted.-

com/we-are-made-to-be-touched-so-what-happens-when-we-arent/

Harvard Health. (2021, December 13). *The power of the placebo effect*. https://www.health.harvard.edu/mental-health/the-power-of-the-placebo-effect

Hyper-Independence and Trauma: What's the Connection? (n.d.). Verywell Mind. https://www.verywellmind.com/hyper-independence-and-trauma-5524773

Kotifani, A. (2022, September 26). *Moai—This Tradition is Why Okinawan People Live Longer, Better*. Blue Zones. https://www.bluezones.com/2018/08/moai-this-tradition-is-why-okinawan-people-live-longer-better/

L. (2022, April 2). *11.3: Four Major Types of Conflict*. Medicine LibreTexts. https://med.libretexts.org/Bookshelves/Nursing/Leadership_and_Influencing_Change_in_Nursing_(Wagner)

Leaf, C. (2021). *Cleaning Up Your Mental Mess: 5 Simple, Scientifically Proven Steps to Reduce Anxiety, Stress, and Toxic Thinking*. Baker Books.

Loneliness and Social Isolation Linked to Serious Health Conditions. (2021, April 30). Www.cdc.gov. https://www.cdc.gov/aging/publications/features/lonely-older-adults.html

Martin, R. (n.d.). *Emotional Intelligence | RocheMartin*. Www.rochemartin.com. https://www.rochemartin.com/emotional-intelligence

Martin, R. (2022, January 12). *50 tips for improving your emotional intelligence*. Www.rochemartin.com. https://www.rochemartin.com/blog/50-tips-improving-emotional-intelligence

McMurray, C. (n.d.). *Why the Brain Loves Stories*. Www.brainfacts.org. Retrieved February 5, 2023, from https://www.brainfacts.org/neuroscience-in-society/the-arts-and-the-brain/2021/why-the-brain-loves-stories-030421

Mindbodygreen. (2022, December 13). *6 Types Of Boundaries You Deserve To Have (And How To Maintain Them)*. Mindbodygreen.

https://www.mindbodygreen.com/articles/six-types-of-boundaries-and-what-healthy-boundaries-look-like-for-each

MindTools | Home. (n.d.). Www.mindtools.com. https://www.mindtools.com/az4wxv7/active-listening

Morin, A. (2015, November 11). *5 Ways Mentally Strong People Deal With Rejection: Rejection hurts, but it doesn't have to hold you back*. Inc. Retrieved March 8, 2023, from https://www.inc.com/amy-morin/5-ways-mentally-strong-people-deal-with-rejection.html

Most of Us Are Touch Starved | Psychology Today. (n.d.). Www.psychologytoday.com. Retrieved February 7, 2023, from https://www.psychologytoday.com/us/blog/emotional-fitness/202109/most-us-are-touch-starved

Murphy, S. (2015). *The Optimistic Workplace: Creating an Environment That Energizes Everyone* (1st ed.). AMACOM.

Nawijn, J., Marchand, M. A., Veenhoven, R., & Vingerhoets, A. J. (2010). Vacationers Happier, but Most not Happier After a Holiday. *Applied Research in Quality of Life*, 5(1), 35–47. https://doi.org/10.1007/s11482-009-9091-9

Onojighofia, T. (2020). Towards a Comprehensive Theory of Love: The Quadruple Theory. *Frontiers in Psychology, 11*. https://doi.org/10.3389/fpsyg.2020.00862

R. (2021, April 12). *The Co-Regulation Effect*. Individual, Couples, and Sex Therapy in Raleigh, NC. https://relationshiprestoration.org/2021/04/12/the-co-regulation-effect/

Reeder, H. (2012, February 7). *Attraction, Just Between Friends: New research reveals what really happens when Harry meets Sally*. Psychology Today. Retrieved March 9, 2023, from https://www.psychologytoday.com/intl/blog/i-can-relate/201202/attraction-just-between-friends

Roberts, T. (2019, August 13). *Echo Chambers and Why They are So Dangerous • Paleo Foundation*. Paleo Foundation. https://paleofoundation.com/why-echo-chambers-are-so-dangerous/

Rose, V. (2022, July 14). *Targeting Conflict Management Techniques in the Workplace - Pollack Peacebuilding Systems*. Pollack Peace-building Systems. https://pollackpeacebuilding.-com/blog/targeting-conflict-management-techniques-in-the-workplace

Santi, J. (n.d.). *The Secret to Happiness Is Helping Others*. https://time.com/collection/guide-to-happi-ness/4070299/secret-to-happiness/

Schutte, N., Malouff, J., & Thorsteinsson, E. (2013). Increasing Emotional Intelligence through Training: Current Status and Future Directions The Nature of Emotional Intelligence. ENSEC, 5(1), 56–72. https://www.um.edu.mt/li-brary/oar/bitstream/123456789/6150/1/vol5i1p4.pdf

Shrikant, A. (2022, September 19). *Why this Stanford researcher says you should ask your friends for more favors: "We are a collaborative society."* CNBC. https://www.cnbc.com/2022/09/17/new-study-you-should-ask-your-friends-for-help-more-heres-why.html

Times, A., & Times, A. (2023, February 18). *Value Conflicts Explained - ADR Times*. ADR Times. https://www.adrtimes.-com/value-conflicts/

The Value Of Shared Experiences | Nurse Next Door. (2019, June 29). Nurse next Door Home Care Services. https://www.nursenextdoor.com.au/blog/the-value-of-shared-experiences

Vilendrer. (2014, July 10). *The Five Main Causes of Conflict*. Vilen-drer Law, PC. https://www.vilendrerlaw.com/five-main-causes-conflict-mediation-can-resolve/

Washington, D. R. (2019, February 19). *How Expectations Influence Performance*. InformED. https://www.opencolleges.e-du.au/informed/features/expectations-influence-performance/

What Are Time Boundaries and How to Set Them Up? (2022, June 2). Week Plan. https://weekplan.net/time-management-boundaries

What is respect in a healthy relationship? - love is respect. (2022, April 25). Love Is Respect. https://www.loveisrespect.org/resources/what-is-respect-in-a-healthy-relationship/

When Conversation Boundaries are Crossed. (n.d.). Candace Smith Etiquette. https://www.candacesmithetiquette.com/conversation-boundaries.html

With Love, C. (2019, April 11). *Words of Affirmation Explained - The 5 Love Languages®.* Crated With Love. https://cratedwithlove.com/blogs/relationship-tips/words-of-affirmation-love-language-explained

Young, K. (2020, August 17). *Vulnerability: The Key to Close Relationships.* Hey Sigmund. https://www.heysigmund.com/vulnerability-the-key-to-close-relationships/